A Whisper Past

Childless after Eugenic Sterilization in Alberta

a memoir by Leilani Muir

The author can be contacted at:
leilani.omalley@gmail.com.

Produced by:

FriesenPress

Suite 300 – 852 Fort Street
Victoria, BC, Canada V8W 1H8

www.friesenpress.com

Distributed to the trade by The Ingram Book Company

TABLE OF CONTENTS

Dedication

To all the children of the world
who have suffered abuse in any way.

Day 1 of the trial of Muir's lawsuit against the Government of Alberta, June 12, 1995; Muir being questioned by her lawyer Jon Faulds

Question: I would like you to just look at one last document, Ms. Muir. Could you look close to the—about in the first third—a third of the way into that binder, document C093?

Answer: Okay.

Q: Can you tell us who wrote that?

A: I did.

Q: Okay. And can you tell us just what you were trying to put down?

A: I was writing down my life history as I could remember it.

Preface: *A Poem Saved My Life*

It has taken me over 20 years to write my story. It was hard to write, because it brought back a lot of bad memories. Being a very private person, I haven't told many of these stories before, but I know now that I was just hurting myself by keeping my stories to myself.

The poem at the end of this preface was the start of this book. In 1988 it came out of nowhere while I was living in Victoria and helped me turn my life around. I'd never written poetry in my life, but God was at my shoulder that day, helping me write down the words. I should have been dead many times because of the way my mother treated me, but He saved me. After I wrote the poem, I decided to get help instead of ending my life. I phoned the local mental health clinic. A nurse named Myra answered and talked to me for a very long time. She said she wanted me to come in and meet someone very nice, a doctor called Mike Kovacs. It took her a while to convince me, but I said, "Yes."

For most of my life, I felt worthless. When I was growing up, people called me a 'moron.' Up until the day I walked into the clinic, I couldn't bring myself to talk about my full story. Now that I know I have something worthwhile to say, I want to get my story out to other people, and I want to tell kids that there's always somebody who will hear them; they just have to find that person.

I thank God for the people who came into my life that day in December of 1988. After visiting the clinic, I knew I wouldn't have to be quiet any longer. My mother, who had tried to control me for so many years, was still alive then, but she didn't know about the book. By the time she died three years later, there was no stopping me. I continued writing everything down in preparation for my 1995 sterilization lawsuit. At the beginning, I wrote long hand. Later, I taught myself how to use a computer. I wrote when I felt up to it and as I remembered things. I gave a copy of the first draft to my lawyers, who used it to prepare for the trial. At that time, my story wasn't read out loud in court or photocopied by journalists like the other exhibits in my trial. It was private.

While getting this book ready for publication, I and my editors reviewed the transcripts of the trial and chose several excerpts to be included in the book. This is the first time this material has been made available to the public. The excerpts present testimony from key witnesses who were either involved in my past or knew about the history of eugenics in Alberta. Some of those people were present during the province's shameful sterilization program.

After the trial ended in 1996, I finally felt like sharing my private story with the world. I started writing again. So many times I had second thoughts about this because of my family; I was so worried that they would try to stop me if they found out what I was doing.

I also wrote this book because I want people to know about the terrible things that happened in Canada because of the Alberta sterilization law—our dark, dark history. After I went public just before the trial, people all over the world started talking about sterilization. The media paid attention and started to publish stories about it. In 1996, the National Film Board of Canada released a documentary about the trial. There were also write-ups in Sweden, China, England, and France. I was so pleased that my case helped others talk about their own experiences. Since the trial, I've talked to audiences across North America and overseas in France. Today, universities and colleges across the world use the story of my sterilization and lawsuit to teach the history of Alberta's eugenics program.

In publishing this book, I also hope to help badly treated people, especially children, who are scared for their lives and afraid to speak out. Children are the most vulnerable when it comes to being abused; they're often too afraid to tell anyone about it. That's such a shame! Who is going to believe these things coming from a younger person? I was in my 40s before I started talking about it.

By now, a lot of people have heard about the legal side of this story, but they don't know about MY story. For an update on my story, please check my new website leilanimuir.ca where I have a blog that gives the latest information.

Who Is My Friend?

Look up in the sky and what will you see?

A million stars looking at me.

So you say again who is my friend?

Well, all those stars are Angels

And they are my friends.

The LORD has got all the Angels' hands in his.

And looking down on me and saying,

"These are your friends."

Look into the stars and what will you see?

All the stars in the galaxy.

These are your friends

And always will be.

Thank you Lord, for looking over me.

Leilani Marietta Muir

December, 1988

Victoria, British Columbia, Canada

Friends who examined a preliminary version of the manuscript wondered how a person who was raised in a home for mentally defective children could then write an entire book. The short answer to this question is that Leilani Muir is not now and never was mentally defective, and she should never have been confined in the Provincial Training School for Mental Defectives in Alberta in the first place. The judge at her trial recognized this fact and awarded her damages for being wrongfully confined and stigmatized as a moron.

Because of that terrible situation, a normal child became an insider in a mental institution and is now able to convey to us what life was like there in the 1950s. She tells us what it was like to be taken in front of the stern faces of the Alberta Eugenics Board and then sterilized by two minimally qualified physicians under the guise of having her appendix removed. The agony of her many later attempts to have the sterilization operation reversed is apparent in her personal story.

One feature of Muir's personality helps to explain how she could write a book. She is very stubborn. She never gives up. It was eight years from when her lawsuit was started until she finally won the case in court in 1996. She wanted an apology from the Government of Alberta more than she wanted money, and she took her cause to the Government of Premier Ralph Klein and finally got her apology from him in person when she and a BBC film crew confronted him at a shopping mall in Edmonton during an election campaign. It took another 17 years after the trial with many twists and turns in the journey to finally get this book into print.

I worked with Muir during all 17 years of the journey and am thrilled and relieved to see that she has reached this goal. It is an immense achievement to create such a book despite the difficulties she experienced as a child, then as a young woman set free on the streets of Edmonton, and even after she won her lawsuit. The finishing touches were done to this book while she was facing eviction from the home where she had been living for 16 years.

Doug Wahlsten, Professor Emeritus, University of Alberta

1940

July 15, 1944 ● Born in Calgary, Alberta

1950

← Hospitalized for malnutrition & TB
← Mother applies to send Leilani to PTS
July 12, 1955 ← Admitted to Provincial Training School
Nov. 22, 1957 ← Eugenics Board hearing
1960 Jan. 19, 1959 ← Sterilization operation

PTS

March 9, 1965 ← Taken from PTS by mother
← First marriage
← Divorce

1970

← Repeal of Sexual Sterilization Act

1980 May 2, 1980 ← Second marriage (Muir)

Victoria

← Breakup of marriage

Feb. 24, 1989 ← Treated for depression; IQ test score 89
1990 ← Start of legal action in Victoria

Lawsuit

June 12, 1995 ← Trial begins in Edmonton
← Wins lawsuit; decision by J. Veit

2000

← 1st draft of book completed
← SSHRCC grant:Living Archives of Eugenics
2010 ← 2nd draft of book completed

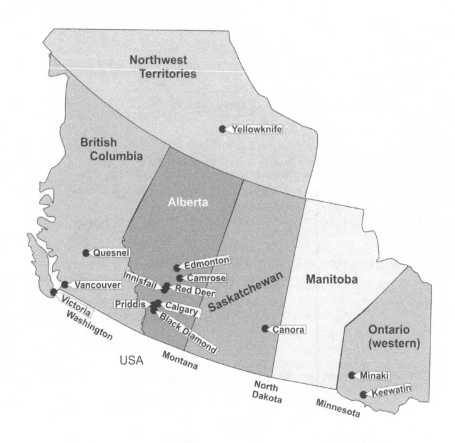

PART ONE

SURVIVING MY MOTHER (1944 – 1955)

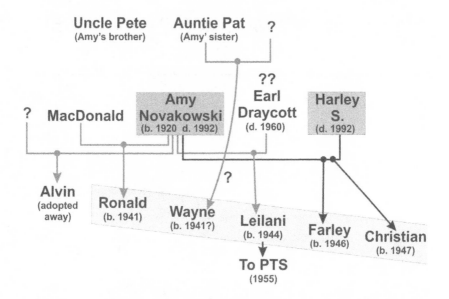

This is the beginning of my life, as best I can remember. Some of these memories are pretty vague, and some of the things I was told growing up weren't true. It took me years to figure out who my real family was. Even now, some of the details are not certain.

The first thing I can clearly recall is living on a farm in Black Diamond, Alberta, where on many days there was a lot of snow. There the man I believed was my father, Harley Scorah was the village constable. He used to come home wearing a uniform. He also worked at farming. The farming started when I was very young. We grew crops: wheat, flax, and other grains. All of us kids worked on the farm. We moved around a lot but always lived on farms. After giving up farming, Harley worked at a number of labour-type jobs - mining coal and driving trucks. We never had a lot of money.

At that time, I lived with people I believed to be my mother, father, and four brothers, but later I learned that this was not quite true. My mother was my real mother. The others, I'm not so sure.

I do know this: I was born in the Calgary General Hospital in Calgary, Alberta, Canada on July 15, 1944 at 6:00 PM. I weighed all of two pounds, four ounces, but I was determined to live! There are no medical records about my birth. I tried to retrieve them later on, but couldn't find any from before 1960. Back in those days, you weren't expected to live when you were born prematurely, but I believe God had plans for me, so he let me live. My older brothers said that, after I was born, I slept on the oven door in a wooden orange box, wrapped in cloth diapers and cotton batting. I had a nice warm bed for a while.

I was 10 years old before I found out that my first and middle names were Leilani Marietta. This is the only good thing my mother ever did for me—she gave me two good names!

BIG SURPRISE AT VITAL STATISTICS OFFICE

For the first 20 years of my life, I believed that my birth father's name was Harley Scorah and that my mother's name was Amy May Ann Scorah. At least that is what I was told. I was the only daughter in a family of five kids. Although I was known as Scorah, I didn't find out until I was in my 20s that official documents referred to me as

Leilani Draycott. I learned this when I wanted to get married for the first time and went to a Vital Statistics office to get my birth certificate. I told the man at the office that my name was "Leilani Scorah." I sure was surprised when they told me, "Your name's not Scorah. It says 'Draycott' on your birth certificate." "That's funny," I said, "because I've never known any other name but Scorah." Earl Bertram Draycott was in fact registered as my birth father. I never met Draycott, and my mother never said anything about him to me. This news came as a big shock, because Harley Scorah was the only father that any of us knew, even my oldest brother Ron. After that, I began checking other things out for myself.

During that same visit to Vital Statistics, I found out that my mother's maiden name was Novakowski. She said she was born on the ship that brought her parents from Poland to Canada. I never saw her birth or marriage certificates, and I don't know if she ever changed her name legally to Draycott. As I found out later, my mother and Draycott got married in 1941 before he joined the army and went to Europe in 1942 to fight in the war. He must have been overseas when I was born in 1944. In the end, I really do not know who my birth father was; my mother told us so many lies.

I also discovered that my mother and Harley Scorah did not get married until the 1960s, although they had been living together as man and wife for as long as any of us kids could remember. When she began living with my stepfather Harley Scorah, she took his last name as hers, probably to look respectable. This was because my mother was still legally married to Draycott and never got divorced when he came back from the war. Earl Draycott was killed in 1960 in a car accident in Canora, Saskatchewan, while riding with his mother and a man who was said to be his brother. They were hit by a truck, apparently after the driver had a heart attack at the wheel. After Draycott died, my mother and Harley Scorah were finally legally married.

My mother had one sister, Auntie Pat (Patricia Michelle), who died of cancer in the early 1950s. I only remember meeting her once, when I was about four or five years old. We were in the car and she was driving. I got to wear some of her clothes because she was so tiny. Auntie Pat lived in Ontario and had a step-brother, Uncle Pete who lived in Saskatchewan.

FIVE BROTHERS, SEVERAL FATHERS

Growing up, I had four brothers. Ronald (Ron) was born in 1941. His birth certificate lists his father as McDonald, a man who was said to have been an RCMP officer. Wayne was about the same age as Ron and may have been Auntie Pat's boy. I only know this because I once overheard Wayne say he was our cousin. This is all I know about it. Auntie Pat had a son named Donny who we were told was our cousin. To see our cousin Donny together with Wayne, you'd say they were twins, except Donny had dark hair and Wayne had blond hair. So I don't know for sure who Wayne's mother and father were, but he was raised by my mother from when he was about 10 days old and always went by the name Scorah. Farley was born in 1946. He and my youngest brother, Christian (Chris), have Harley Scorah named as the father on their birth certificates.

Later on, we found out that we had another brother, Alvin. My mother said he was a twin brother to Ron, and she told us for years that Alvin died by drowning in a pig trough when he was four. All those years, my stepfather, my brothers, and I always believed Alvin was dead. At one point, I even went to the graveyard where our mother said he had been laid to rest, but I never found his grave. In the 1980s, we found out why. Alvin had been adopted by a family of German immigrants when he was two. He was either given up for adoption or taken away from our mother before 1941.

My brothers and I were really surprised when Alvin came looking for his birth mother. Apparently he had been looking for our family for years. He was trying to get in touch with Uncle Pete in Saskatchewan in 1986, when he ran into Uncle Pete one day almost by chance. Alvin was dying of cancer and must have known it, because he died in December of that same year. I met him only once. He was curious about where he came from.

So, Alvin was my oldest brother. We don't know who his father was. Alvin was older than Ron by a couple of years. That was even before my mother met Scorah or McDonald. She was married to Draycott until he left for the war. My stepfather, Harley Scorah, wouldn't have known Alvin was still alive, because Alvin was not in our home by the time Harley and my mother got together. After Alvin died, I never saw his family again. He was about 47 years old when he died. He left a wife and five children behind: two girls and three boys. I wish I had known Alvin was alive so we could have gotten to know each other. We'll meet again some day in heaven.

This is how I ended up with five brothers. The kids in my family were, from oldest to youngest: Alvin, Ron, Wayne, myself, Farley, and Chris.

MISSING GRANDPARENTS

I never knew my grandparents' names on my mother's side or on my stepfather's side. All I remember of my dad's mother is that she used to knit me dresses with the pants attached. They were so beautiful. I remember a yellow one and a lilac-coloured dress which was my favourite. I didn't get to wear them more than one time, though, because I almost never got to be with people other than family or wear nice clothes.

I met my mother's parents only once when we were staying with them in Saskatchewan. I was maybe five years old. Because I was hungry and given very little food, I got up one night and took a loaf of homemade bread. I hollowed it and ate the inside. Then I put the crust back so no one would know until they went to get some bread. My grandmother saw it first but never said anything to my mother, and I didn't get a beating for it. My grandmother must have known that something was terribly wrong for me to do that.

My mother's father's funeral was held in Canora, Saskatchewan. I was six or seven years old and still living at home at the time, but I was not allowed to go. When I look at the picture (at the start of the next chapter) from my grandfather's funeral, I regret that I didn't get to know my grandmother and grandfather or Uncle John. My mother kept me away from them my whole life, except for one time when I was at my grandma and grandpa's place in Saskatchewan. This is the only photograph I have of my grandmother and grandfather, or of my family from when I was a girl. It was given to me by Uncle Pete and his wife, Aunt Kassie, when I was visiting them several years after my mother died. The photograph shows my grandfather, my mother's father, in the casket. The older lady in the picture is my grandmother. The boy is my brother Farley, and the woman with her hand on his shoulder is my mother, standing beside her brother, my Uncle John. I do not know the man standing on the right.

Grandparents are supposed to be very special people in a child's life. This wasn't so in my life. What a shame it was to be kept away from my grandparents this way. Grandparents can be the glue that holds a child's life together. I will get to know all of my grandparents, aunts and uncles, and all those who should have been in my life but were not. I believe very strongly that we will meet again in heaven.

This is what I know of my family. It's confusing, and it took me a long time to understand, so a family tree is shown here to help.

There are no photographs of me from my childhood. Any time a family photo was taken, I was left out. The old picture of the funeral is all I have, and I am not in it.

This chapter was so very difficult to write because it brought back many memories of terrible times in my past. It will not be easy for other people to read, either. Some people may want to skip the details and move on. I did the same thing with my life. But I decided to write down exactly what happened to me, so that others could know and I could come to grips with my past, or at least try to understand it.

I was very young when my mother started to be cruel to me. I guess this is how I realized she didn't want me around or in my family's life. She never did say why. Living with her was a trial and I'm very lucky to have survived.

I don't know anything about my mother's childhood or what she went through as a child. It felt like she was taking out on me all of her anger about whatever was upsetting her so much in life. She was a very sick person indeed to treat a child so cruelly.

One thing I know for sure is that my mother didn't want a girl. She told me this many times. To this day, I don't know why she didn't put me up for adoption when I was born. My mother kept me hidden, like a secret. A lot of people who knew my parents and four brothers didn't even know there was a daughter. I tried so hard to be the kind of daughter and sister that the whole family could be proud of, but to them, I was an outsider, I was an invisible child.

A GIRL CALLED "TOM"

Until I turned 21 years old, my family never called me by my real name. Instead of Leilani, they just called me "Tom." This was an everyday thing, even with my brothers. They learned this from my mother. At the time, there was a farm hand named Tom working for my parents. One day, my mother caught him giving me some fruit. When I went back in the house, she beat me and said, "If you want to talk to Tom, well, from now on we'll call you Tom." It was "Tom, do this," and "Tom, do that." The only time they didn't call me Tom was when other people were around, or when we were out. Then they called me "Marie," which isn't my name either. So I went with whatever name I was called at the time. I didn't know any better. At school the teachers and students called me "Marie." I didn't know my real name until I was put into the institution when I was 11. There, for the first time, the nurses called me Leilani.

My mother never really spoke to me unless she was screaming at me to do something. I cried a lot on the inside because, if my mother heard me cry, she yelled, "Shut up and stop crying!" Even when she was beating the heck out of me, I wasn't supposed to cry. So I learned to cry without making a sound while the tears ran down my face.

Sometimes my mother said, "Don't say a word to anyone else, you hear me?" I was too scared to talk back or tell anyone about the abuse because I would pay for it if I did. I always had to keep a straight and solemn face. When someone was visiting, I was not allowed to talk, so I couldn't tell anyone what was happening to me. I didn't dare tell, because someone might tell my mother. My mother never mistreated me in any way when other people were watching; she just had to give me "that look" and I shut up. My mother's cruelty towards me was like a craziness. I believe there was some kind of monster in this woman.

UNLOVED, UNWANTED

I wanted so much to please her, for her to be proud of me. This never happened. I desperately wanted someone to love me. I just wanted my mother to hold me and be nice to me because I was her little girl. How very much I longed for my mother's acceptance.

Not a day went by that I wasn't beaten with a belt, a stick, a board, or even a hammer. After every beating, she continued to eat, cook, bake, or spend time with the rest of the family, play cards or whatever. She would act like she had done nothing wrong. It was like she was programmed to be cruel to me. She never seemed to feel any remorse for it. This happened to me from the time I was a baby until I was 21 years old.

MOTHER'S FAVOURITES

My brothers weren't treated like this. They ran around having fun It seemed that my oldest brother, Ron, could do nothing wrong. From the time I was a young child, I saw how my mother favoured him. He was momma's boy. Whenever Ron wanted something like money or a car or anything, Mom found a way to get it for him. Whenever his marriages broke up, oh Lord behold, my mom always found a way to blame the wife! Yet I watched him bully his wives and hit his kids. When his daughter Sherry was two years old, I gave her a nickel. She was so happy when she got it that she ran to show it to her dad. Instead of giving her a hug and saying "go put it in your bank," he slapped it out of her tiny hand. She started to cry, so he smacked her on the head and told her to go to her room. When I went to say something to him about what he had done, he told me to shut up. So I gave him a dirty look and slammed the door so hard I think I cracked it. He treated his own family members so badly. The apple doesn't fall far from the tree, does it?

Ron was my mother's favourite until he went to jail in August of 1984 for shooting and killing three people. My mother phoned me and said that Ron had shot and killed his wife Kara, her mother and one of her sons. The family had been living in Saskatchewan, but finally Kara left Ron and moved to Delta, BC, to live with her mother. Ron followed her to BC, bringing loaded guns with him. I could not believe my ears and knew my mother often lied, so I phoned the Vancouver police, and they said it was true.

After the shooting, my two youngest brothers Chris and Farley took Ron's place as my mother's favourites.

MOTHER'S PUNCHING BAG

The beatings and the yelling were the only communications my mother had with me. She needed a punching bag and I was it. One time when my mother was in bed, the phone rang. She told me to answer it and ask who it was, so I did as I was told. After she got off the phone, you'd think I'd committed a crime or something. She beat me really bad. There was a doorknob on the kitchen table. She picked it up and hit me on the head with it and it cut my head open. She cut me so badly that she had to shave around the cut to clean it. She made me take a bath to clean off the blood. When my dad came home, she told him I fell down the basement stairs. To cover up her lie, that day she even let me eat, which really surprised me. She was very good at playing those games.

The fingers on both of my hands now have swollen, misshapen knuckles. This came from having them broken time and time again by my mother. She was such a bully; she could have been Hitler's sister! She slammed windows down on my hands, smashed them with a rolling pin, or stabbed them with a knife or fork, whatever she had at the time. One of the most painful things she did was bend my fingers to the back of my hand. To this day, every time I look at them, I remember the pain I had to endure for so many years. I don't ever remember seeing a doctor about any of this. I still had to do chores with broken fingers. Trying to carry wood and stack it in neat piles was very hard when I was in so much pain.

COLD AND PAIN

The only time I was allowed to sleep in a proper bed was when we lived in Keewatin, Ontario. I was there for a while one summer when I was 14 or 15 years old and slept in a cot. Neighbours lived close by and dropped in quite often, so my mother put on a false front, as she always did with people outside the family.

For most of my childhood, though, I slept on the porch of our house, in sheds, and in granaries, where there was no heat whatsoever. Because of the cold and for fear of being locked in those places, I wet myself most nights. The urine froze to the only blanket I had, and I slept on that same wet blanket all night. My mother made me wash everything in cold water, and in the winter it wouldn't be dry by nighttime. It was different in the summer. We didn't have a dryer at the time, so we hung everything to dry on a clothesline outside.

In the granary, I went to the bathroom on the floor in one of the corners. From the time when I was about five years old, my mother rolled me up in a blanket and tied me up so I couldn't get out of bed in the middle of the night to go to the bathroom, or get something to eat. The next morning she put salt between my legs and she said, "Now pee yourself again." It hurt so much.

When I was little, I used to dirty my pants too. I asked to go to the bathroom and my mother yelled at me to hold it. Of course I couldn't hold it forever, so I dirtied myself and she rubbed the dirty pants in my face.

I dreaded sleeping in the granary because I was scared every time I heard a noise. But in another way I felt safe, because my mother wasn't there. When I was alone in those places, I often thought, "Why can't I sleep in a bed like my brothers do? Why can't I? And why can't I sit at the table and eat with everyone else?" During the day, I sometimes fell asleep in the hay because it was the only way I could get warm and get some rest. If I was found sleeping there, I got a beating. When I was able to sleep at night, I often wished I could sleep forever.

ISOLATION

In this way, I experienced years and years of isolation. When people came to our house, my mother hid me away either in the granary or in the barn, or I wasn't allowed to speak to anyone. I never felt safe, no matter who was at our house. I heard them in the kitchen or the living room eating and laughing, or playing cards or some kind of game. I asked myself, "Why won't you let me be in there having fun with all of you?" If I was allowed to be in the same room with the others, which wasn't often, I had to stand over to one side of the room and not say a word to anyone. I was so shy and scared. I couldn't win, no matter what I did. I was trapped in this cage with my mother's furious hatred for me.

I didn't have any friends and was never allowed outside to play. I have always felt unworthy of being close to anyone. Even now, it seems like I'm always doing something to push everyone away from me.

OCCASIONAL SCHOOLING

Although my mother tried very hard to hide me and keep me away from other people, it was the law in Alberta that children should go to school at the age of five, so I sometimes went to school to keep my mother out of trouble. I don't remember much about school or teachers. By the time I was 10, I had only reached a grade two level. This wasn't because I couldn't learn in school; it was because I wasn't often allowed to go to school. As soon as someone started questioning my family, we'd move.

I attended school when we lived in the towns of Innisfail, Black Diamond, and Priddis, Alberta. Those villages were tiny and had one-room schools, with all the grades together in one classroom. We always walked to school from our farms. My mother never gave me a lunch to take with me, so I sometimes stole other kids' lunches. Once, after catching me taking someone else's lunch, one of my teachers started to bring me food. It was so good to have my own lunch, and to not have to steal.

I kept to myself at recess while my brothers and all the other kids were playing and having fun. If I did play with other kids, my brothers told my mother about it, and I got a beating and couldn't go to school the next day. Then she said, "I told you not to play at school or talk to anyone." She was so scared I would tell the other children or the teacher something bad about her.

To stay out of trouble, I always tried to be good in school. I got into enough trouble at home! Once, because my brothers dared me to, I threw the teacher's strap in the river behind the school. I guess they thought that the teacher, Mrs. Wonnacot, wouldn't punish me for it because she wouldn't believe that it was me who did it. As they had guessed, she took her belt and used it on some of the other kids.

CHORES AND MORE CHORES

I don't know of any children today who can cook, wash clothes, or iron before they are eight years old. Years ago, young girls had to learn these things because it was a necessity. In my case, it was as a result of my mother's cruelty that I had to learn to do them at such a young age. From the age of five, I had to wash clothes and floors, cook breakfast, and then go out and clean the barns.

One day when I was very young, maybe five or six years old, I fainted. When I came to, there was light green paint everywhere. My mother was painting a room and had made me hold the paint can up in the air so she could paint the ceiling and the walls. Being under-fed, holding the paint, and smelling the fumes, I just couldn't take any more. Needless to say, I was made to clean up the spilled paint. It's sort of funny to me now, because my mother didn't have enough paint to finish the rest of the room after this.

My mother used her foot to get me up and out of bed. I had to clean the barn by washing all the stalls out with Lysol, then carry wood and bring it close to the house. I stacked a lot of wood in the summers, getting ready for winter. After finishing the outside work, I worked in the house making beds, ironing laundry and washing dishes. By then, my mother had already put all the food away and rinsed the dishes before I washed them, so I wouldn't eat any food off them.

"DAD" GAVE NO HELP

For all those years, no one in my family tried to put a stop to the cruelty that was going on in our house. Whenever Harley was out of the house, the beatings got worse. Many times, when my mother was brutalizing me, he left the room and worked outside. He never once intervened. As a young child, I asked myself, "Why? Why, daddy? Why won't you stop mom from being mean to me and always hurting me?" No one ever tried to stop her, because my mother was a cruel person and they must have all been afraid of her. My brothers were also scared of her, even if they didn't say so. Only God was there to help me.

I tried to run away when I was about eight or nine years old. I ran from the house and hid in the field. My stepdad was cutting the wheat down. When he almost ran me over, I jumped up and scared the heck out of him. He never spanked or beat me for that. He just told me never to do it again, and he shared his lunch with me. This was the only time that I got to ride with my dad on his tractor.

Harley was never mean to any of us kids. I wish he had left my mother and taken me with him. My mother was mean to him too. She made him a broken man. Her cruel words and treatment made him that way. She always had to control everyone, and my stepfather was no exception. He was a very quiet man and never raised his voice to anyone, even though my mother shouted and shouted at him all the time. She didn't use profanities, but her words were nasty and full of hate. He never argued with her and always did what she wanted. She never hit him, though. In fact, I never saw any kind of physical contact between them. They never hugged, cuddled, or kissed in front of me. And she never said anything nice or sweet to him that I can recall.

THEIR MOTHER'S SONS

Seeing our mother always treating me so cruelly, my two older brothers did the same. Whenever they got mad at someone, they took it out on me. Whenever I went to talk, they'd say "Shut up. You don't know what you're talking about. You're retarded." My brothers did many things to hurt me, like throwing rocks at my feet to make me dance, as they called it, or shooting gooseberries at me with homemade bean-shooters. Those gooseberries were really hard. Many times my face, arms, and legs hurt so badly.

When I was seven to nine years old, my brothers built forts out of snow at the bottom of a hill. Then they put me inside a big tractor tire and rolled me in it down the hill toward the snow forts. I was so small that I couldn't do anything to stop it until it bumped into the forts and came to a fast stop. My youngest brother, Chris, hadn't been born when most of this was happening to me, but he made up for it later. When he was nine years old, he started following the others and kicked me in the legs and did other mean things.

COLD

I know very well what it's like to be cold. I had to go outside in the middle of the winter with no mitts on my hands, no hat or scarf to keep my head or ears warm, and no winter boots, just a cast-off pair of boys' shoes. Those shoes were always too big for me. I thought I would never know what warmth was. In the summer, I didn't have any shoes whatsoever to wear.

When the snow was deep and the weather very cold, my mother sent me outside and made me run from the house to the barns and back to make paths through the snow for everyone else to walk on. When she let me back in the house, she said, "If you're cold, get in the corner and kneel down." She sprinkled some wheat kernels on the floor in the corner of the room and ordered me to kneel on them. Wheat kernels are very hard, like little stones. I was usually wearing a dress and there was no protection on my skinny knees, so the kernels really hurt. She had many little ways of doing things like this and usually hurt me in some way every day.

HUNGER

Besides the cold, hunger was something I also knew well. My stomach hurt because I was always hungry; my mother didn't give me food for days on end. Everyone else in the family got lunches or regular meals. My mother fed herself, my stepfather, and my brothers, while I stood close to the table and watched everyone else eat. To make it worse, they said things like, "Mmmm, it's so good," or "Can I have more" or "I'm not able to eat any more," while I stood by starving. Other times, I was forced to stand facing the corner so they wouldn't have to see my face. If I tried to ask for something to eat, my mother knocked me around and told me to never ask for food again.

STEALING TO SURVIVE

I learned at a very early age to steal food to keep alive. When my mother and father went out somewhere, my mother counted any food she could before they left. If my brothers ate something, my mother asked them where it went. Instead of saying they ate it, they blamed me and said, "Tom ate it." Of course, I got another beating. This was an everyday occurrence. My mother even taped a cowbell to the fridge so she could hear the door open. If my brothers took something to eat, she didn't say a word, but if I tried to get anything to eat out of the fridge, the world would come to an end!

I always found a way to get food. I ate wheat from the granary—it made really good gum. Whenever I could, I took vegetables from the garden in the summer, carrots or peas, something I could wash off and eat really fast, then give the tops and pea pods to the pigs. Once in a while, I'd take pickles from the crock-pot in the shed, but only two at a time so no one would notice they were missing. I don't recall ever being given a glass of water at home. I drank rainwater when it rained and, in the wintertime, I ate as much snow as I could.

One night, somebody was staying over at our place, so my mother didn't tie me up. I snuck into the kitchen and took some wieners. For once, I knew what it was like to have a full stomach! The next morning, I got rid of the wiener wrapper and was outside before my mother got up. I never got caught that time. Whenever I stole food, I had to eat it right away and in a hurry. I couldn't hide it for later on, because I was scared my mother would find it.

Many times I had to eat out of a pig trough. If my mother had found out about it, she would probably have made sure I was never outside again when the pigs were being fed.

Please understand that my mother was not against all stealing. She was against *me* stealing food. I saw her teach my little brothers how to steal from the grocery store. In the winter they wore bulky snowsuits and they kept the suits on while my mother was shopping. At the meat counter, she slipped a roast of beef into an unzipped snowsuit, then zipped it up so the lady at the checkout could not see it. When they got home, out came that roast, and everyone but me had a fine dinner.

As a child, as a young adult, and as a woman now, I've always asked myself and God: "Why doesn't my mother love me or talk to me like a human being, and stop treating me like I'm nothing, like I have no right to be here on this earth? What did I do wrong to make her hate me so much from the time of my birth on? Did my mother give up on herself? If she did, did she know why? Could anyone have helped her?" These questions have troubled me for most of my life. My mother sometimes drank alcohol when we were children, but I know this isn't an excuse for what she did to me.

I never hated my mother, because that's not my way. Hate is such a powerful word. I don't believe in it. I loved her, no matter what, even when she tried her very best to break me down. I often worried I'd turn out to be cruel just like her, but I didn't. Although I was my mother's prisoner for so many years, I always believed I'd make something of myself. As a very young girl, I fantasized that I was in a big house with lots of dolls and animals, with a mother and father who wrapped me in big white fur coats. I had food of every kind and more candy than even a candy store, and a lot of love from my mother and father.

LASTING PAIN OF REJECTION

You can't get rid of the hurt of being rejected by your parents. I know I didn't do anything wrong, but I also wonder what I could have done to make my mother love and want me. As the years passed and I grew older, I dreamt that my mother was a queen and I was her little princess, that she never hurt me again, and that my brothers and I lived in a perfect home.

I believe one reason my mother treated me like she did was because I reminded her of her sister, Auntie Pat. I even looked like her. My Auntie Pat was only 32 when she died from cancer. Once when I was home for a holiday when 17 years old, my Uncle John came to my parents' home. When Uncle John saw me for the first time in a long while, he called me Pat. My mother said, "That's not Pat. It's Leilani." He said I looked so much like her. This didn't make my mother happy. I'll never know if my mother was really angry at me all those years, or at her sister.

"Mrs. Scorah was very definite that she didn't want Leilani."

From report by W.E. Alford, Provincial Training School matron, July 30, 1964 ("Muir vs. Alberta," trial transcript, p. 241)

When my mother visited in later years when I was an adult, I sat and listened to her run other people down. The lies never stopped. Even when I was in my 40's, my mother was cruel to me. She didn't beat me, but she was verbally abusive and still very mean. She never stopped hating and being so jealous of others.

Everyone in my family except my stepfather treated me like I was nobody, like someone they wished hadn't been born. Being told that I was stupid and retarded all the time cut very deeply.

So here's what I have to say to anyone reading this book: Please think before you speak harsh words to anyone - family members, friends, and anyone you love - because you can never take the words back once you've spoken them.

A SWIFT END TO THE ABUSE

My mother and Harley Scorah continued to live together until 1965 when they split up. Harley moved to a little town in British Columbia. I saw him once as an adult, when I was living in Victoria. Even though he was in his sixties at the time, he looked more like he was 85. He was OK the day I saw him, but after that he became very ill with heart problems. I phoned him to show concern about his health, but he told me I was like my mother because I kept phoning him.

Harley died of heart failure in the summer of 1992, at the age of 65. My mother died that same year. She was 72 and living on a pension. One of my brothers phoned me with the news. My mother had been living common-law with Mike Kozak in Wildwood, Alberta for several years. Although she had been suffering from cancer, she died within four hours of having a heart attack. Mike settled her affairs and dealt with her possessions.

It's strange to me that Mike had her body cremated before we even knew she'd passed away. Only her ashes were there in an urn at the funeral. I attended the service in Wildwood along with my brothers. They showed no emotion at all; not one of them even shed a tear as far as I could see. With me, it was different. I walked to the front of the chapel and knelt before the picture of my mother to say goodbye. It was silent in the room. I asked her out loud why she hated me so much, why she had not loved me. Then I broke down and wept for a long time, letting out years of pain and hurt. My brother Christian finally came up, knelt beside me, and tried to comfort me, but I just couldn't stop crying. I was the only one who wept openly for her, even after all the terrible things she did to me. She was my mother and I loved her, even though she never loved me.

My mother died without a will or an apology. She left no documents or old photos either, as far as I know. The only thing I got that was hers was through my Uncle Pete a couple of years before he died, just as I was getting to know him. He gave me some pictures that I now have in my album.

I wanted to contact him for years before that, but my mother told me not to go near him. I knew of Uncle Pete and his wife Aunt Kassie, but hadn't seen them since I was 10 or 11. Aunt Kassie remembers hearing about my parents having a daughter, but she never saw me while I was a girl when they visited the house. This is because my mother hid me away when people came over. I even remember being asked to hide under the stairs, then peeking out to see who was visiting.

When I returned to Victoria after my mother's funeral, I felt better in a way because I knew my mother could no longer hurt me by beating me or by her mean words. *I was finally free.* If she hadn't died when she did, I would never have gone to trial; I was still very scared of my mother even though I rarely saw her after I moved to Victoria.

In this chapter and for most of my life, I have struggled to understand why my mother hated me so much and taught my brothers to be cruel to me too, but it makes no sense. There is nothing in her background or during the years I lived with her that justifies her actions towards me. She could never explain her hatred for me to my face. Now she has had to answer to God for her deeds.

My mother first started trying to get rid of me when I was about seven years old. Sometimes, when I was a very young child, my family left me home alone while they went out. Once, when I was seven or eight and we were living in Priddis, my mother locked me in a room by myself all day and all night. I didn't have any food, water, heat, or light. It was winter, and it was so cold. I can still feel the cold as I'm writing this down. My family came home late that night. I was very, very sick.

They took me from Priddis to the Crippled Children's Hospital in Calgary right away. I still wonder what made my mother take me to the hospital that day, after being so cruel to me for so many years. Maybe she just wanted to wash her hands of me for good. I didn't know then that this trip saved my life. At the hospital, I was put in isolation for a long time. My family never visited me. My arms and legs were taped to boards with needles in my arms. My arms had large sores on them. My mother told me that I had tuberculosis of the bones, but I think I was also suffering from severe malnutrition and pneumonia. Again, it was by the grace of God that I survived.

I can't remember how long I was in the hospital. They were very kind to me there. I wanted to stay because I was happy there and could talk with the other girls without being slapped in the mouth. For the first time in my young life, I felt safe. I had food, warmth, and a proper bed. I was able to act like a normal child, to laugh and play with other kids, and just enjoy myself. And my mother wasn't around.

The only time I wasn't happy at the hospital was the one time when I got a swat on my backside from a doctor. I was in a room with three other girls. We were having pillow fights and throwing balloons with water in them at each other. Our room was a mess, but we were having fun. We put our beds on top of each other, but we couldn't get them back down. When the doctor came in to check on us, he wasn't happy with what our room looked like. He gave us five minutes to put our beds back. When he returned, we still didn't have our beds the right way, so he put them down himself and gave each of us a swat on the backside.

Jon Faulds (my lawyer at the trial speaking to the Judge):
".. while she was in (the) hospital, Miss Muir was seen by a psychiatrist (who) had been asked to assess her intellectual

capacity. Your Ladyship will see evidence in the documentary record that his view was that there was 'an emotional
involvement rather than a primary mental deficiency', a
view which was communicated by that psychiatrist to the
Calgary Guidance Clinic .."

("Muir vs. Alberta", trial transcript, p. 14)

When I was discharged from the hospital, the doctor gave me a
rubber toy, a Pluto dog, as a going-away present. On the way home
from the hospital, my family went to a concert that two of my brothers
were in. This was the first outing that I can remember going to with
my family. After the concert, my brothers took the Pluto dog from me.
I can remember saying, "It's mine! You can't have it." My stay in the
hospital had given me enough confidence that I felt brave enough to
tell my brothers off. I don't remember getting a beating for it, maybe
because we were with other people. It felt so good to mouth off to my
brothers for once.

After my stay in the hospital, I was sent twice to a Catholic resi-
dence run by nuns for orphans and elderly people, located just outside
of Calgary—the Lacombe Home, Midnapore, in 1952 and in 1955. I
think it was also a convent for the nuns. I don't know why my mother
sent me there, or what she told the nuns who ran it. I think she just
wanted to get me out of her house. I was happy there, and the nuns
were very nice to me. It was one hundred percent different from being
at home. We wore clean dresses and went to school every day. When I
had my first communion, they dressed me in white fur. I ate well and
even gained some weight.

I can remember getting some brown liquid medicine while I was there. It tasted awful. It was given to me because I wet my bed at night. I did this until I was about 14 years old, not because I was lazy, but because my nerves were shot, and I was scared so much of the time.

At the trial I learned that my mother decided to get rid of me when I was only 8 years old. First she sent me to the Lacombe Home and convent, then to the Provincial Training School in Red Deer. I wish my mother had left me in the convent. I didn't realize then that she had actually given me away each time I was away from home. The next time she threw me away, it was for 10 years.

PART TWO

LIFE IN THE INSTITUTION (1955-1965)

Chapter 5: *Discarded at the Doorstep*

My mother first applied to have me admitted to the Provincial Training School for Mental Defectives (PTS) in Red Deer in 1953, after I returned home from my first hospital stay, but the application was turned down. I found this out 42 years later, during my trial. We were living in Priddis when I was admitted to the PTS on July 12, 1955. My parents were building a new place. Only the frame was up, so we lived in another house on the same property. The land was given to my stepdad, Harley Scorah, through the DVA (Department of Veterans Affairs) because he had been in the army.

My mother and Harley brought me to the institution three days before my 11th birthday. They didn't tell me where we were going. During the drive there from our home, my parents hid me by making me sit on the floor at my brothers' feet, in the back seat of the car. When they arrived, they stopped the car, left me at the entrance of a large red brick building, and quickly drove away. None of my family members got out to give me a hug or say goodbye. I just remember seeing the smirk on my mother's face as they drove away.

A nurse came out of the building and met me at the bottom of the steps. It was around suppertime, and I saw all those girls the same age as me or older. I was scared, of course, standing there all alone, the other girls staring at me like I was invading their playground. The nurses took me inside a building called Ash Villa and showed me where to sleep. I didn't know it then, but I would live at the PTS for the next 10 years of my life.

Excerpts from admission form for PTS, July 12, 1955

"Age: 10 yrs, 11 mo
Height: 3' 10 ½
Nutrition: fair
Clothing: rather shabby
Amount of money: nil"

When I arrived at the institution, I was wearing a thin white dress, underwear, shoes, but no socks. I was small for my age; the PTS admission form lists me as measuring 3 feet 10 ½ inches tall. The first thing the nurses did when I arrived was to check me from head to toe. They said they'd never seen a child with so many scars on her head. The nurses shaved my head that day. They gave me some nice clothes to wear and toys to play with. At least I could play and have things, not like at home. I got to be a child. That same day, I found out from the nurses that my real name was Leilani, not Tom or Marie, as my family had always called me. I thought Leilani was a beautiful name. But that day I was also given a registration number: I was Trainee #1325.

Jon Faulds (my lawyer speaking on day 1 of the trial): ".. (upon admittance to the PTS) no physician had assisted in the completion of the application form and witnessed it, as the form required. ..the physician's certificate certifying that Miss Muir had been physically examined, that an inquiry had been made into the necessary facts, and that Miss Muir had been found to be mentally defective—a mandatory part of the application form—was blank. It had not been filled out."

("Muir vs. Alberta", trial transcript, p. 13)

I didn't know very much about my new home. At the time, I just thought it was an orphanage, and a safe place away from my home life. The PTS was said to be a "training school" for the disabled, but it really wasn't; it was for both disabled and normal children. There were many other girls and boys there who were like me—children whose parents didn't want them. Although people were supposed to be admitted to the institution based on low intelligence, I wasn't given an IQ test until 1957, two years after I was admitted.

Dr. Copus (psychiatrist who assessed me in 1995): "My
reasons for concern is that there is no clear description of
this child's behavior at the time of her admission. There
is no record of her functioning at school and no attempt
seems to have been made to investigate her home circumstances. The importance of that in my mind is that, if that
had been done, that it may have become more apparent
that, if Ms. Muir's account of her background is accepted
as valid, that there was abuse and depravation [sic] in the
home and that this should have been taken into account as
a possible etiological factor in the reason for her developmental delay."

("Muir vs. Alberta", trial transcript, p. 1159)

BETTER THAN LIFE AT HOME

At the PTS, life was so much better than being with my mother. I
was fed regularly and wasn't beaten up 365 days a year. The only large
drops in weight that I experienced through that period were during
my visits home, where she continued to beat me and deny me food.

For the first few days at the institution, I stayed quietly in my room
or sat in a chair in the playroom. I also attended meals and school. I was
well-trained. I did as I was told for fear I would get a beating if I didn't.
I was scared to do anything, because I was so afraid that my mother
would come, but she never did.

Mostly out of fear, I didn't play with the other kids that first year.
I sat in the playroom, just sat there and watched them play, sat there

watching the door, afraid that any moment my mother might walk in and see me playing and give me a beating for it. I was petrified. It took me almost a year to realize this wouldn't happen, but even then I was still scared and tried to be cautious, because she could come anytime. Once I started to play with other girls, life got better. It felt so good to be able to play and to have toys of my own for the first time in my life. It was so different, being with the other kids, running in the snow with my arms up in the air, not getting a beating every time I turned around. And I was allowed to eat three meals a day. For someone who didn't eat that often at home, it was like going to heaven. I didn't have to go to bed hungry.

At night, I'd have a bath and get into nice, clean pyjamas before going to bed. It was so nice to have my own bed, to sleep in a bed with sheets, blankets and a pillow, and not get tied up in a dirty, stinky blanket. When I was put to bed for the night, I was able to talk to someone and laugh, even when I was supposed to be sleeping. In the middle of the night, I could get up and go to the bathroom, or get a drink of water without stealing it. It was so good to get up in the morning by myself instead of getting kicked out of bed. When we awoke, we had clean clothes to put on—clothes that I didn't have to wash in cold water with my bare hands. I was allowed to sit at a table with others and eat as much as I wanted. It felt so good.

At the PTS, I was also able to go to school, the gym, and outside to play. I learned to ride a bike, skate, and play volleyball and badminton. There was also a television at the PTS; it was the first time I had ever seen one.

The other kids called me "Squirrel." I thought my name was Scorah at the time and we had Squirrel brand peanut butter at the school, so they called me Squirrel instead of Scorah. I was well-liked by many of the nurses, and sometimes received special treatment.

As a small child at home, I never knew what happiness was. I didn't know what it was like getting Christmas or birthday gifts. At 12 years old, while living at the PTS, I celebrated my birthday for the first time and learned that I was born on July 15, 1944. Back at home, there had always been a birthday party for my brothers, but never, ever for me. I recall when my family was living in Keewatin, Ontario, they made a big deal of the fourth birthday for my little brother, Chris. It was two days later than mine. At the institution, I also learned for the first time about Easter, Thanksgiving, and other special holidays.

LIFE IN THE WARDS

The buildings in the institution where the girls lived were named after trees: Birch, Cherry, Oak, and Ash. For boys and men, they were called Pine, Willow, and Spruce, and some of them lived and worked at the farm. Each building was called a villa or ward. Each ward was divided into two parts. There was a row of rooms on each side and a dining room in the middle between the two sides. One side was green and the other yellow. There were eight wards altogether, numbered 1 to 8, with about 50 kids of about the same age in each, 25 on each side of the ward. The younger kids stayed on the first side, and moved to the other side when they got older. Oak Villa, where I lived when older, had two floors in one ward; the lower floor for the tiny kids, the upper for youth 16 and older.

In each ward, there was a playroom, and next to it were our bedrooms and the bathroom. There was also an office, an isolation room, and a sick bay room. The nurses' room was in the office and had windows where they could see into the playroom and the dining room. The matron was always there at night.

Boys and girls were kept apart and never lived in the same villa. We only saw the boys when we went to the gym, had parties, or were at church. I remember having dances on special days when I was 16, at Easter and on Valentine's Day.

In Ash Villa where I first lived, two girls shared each room and we each had our own bed. My first roommate on Ward 1 was Irene. When I was older, they moved me to Oak Ward, where I spent my last two years at the PTS. There, I had a new roommate who became a really good friend. To protect her privacy, I will call her Bobbie Jean. Bobbie Jean and I always had fun together, and are still close friends today.

It was at the PTS that we first heard about Elvis. We saw him on the Ed Sullivan Show and became big fans. My roommate really liked him. We put pictures of Elvis on our closets and walls.

Bobbie Jean was so skinny she had to hang onto walls to walk. She had health problems. After she left the PTS and I was on holiday visiting my parents in Camrose, Alberta, I wrote her a letter a couple of times, but my mother saw them. She took them and scolded me for writing letters. They were never sent to Bobbie Jean.

At the PTS, we were not allowed to seal any letters. The nurses took them to the head office where somebody read them. The letter might or might not be sent on its way. And when we got our mail, it had already been opened and read. Not only that, but while living in Victoria several years later, I learned that many letters and even several packages had been sent to me at the PTS but had not been passed on to me. So, even though the PTS was better than my life at home, in some ways it really was a prison for children.

Aside from the nurses who worked at the PTS, there were matrons who wore uniforms with white dresses and nurse's hats, all starched and stiff. There was one matron for each side of a ward. Miss Soderberg is the first one I can recall on Ward 1, and later there was Miss Schmidt. At Oak Villa, one matron was Miss Alfred. None of the matrons ever shouted at us girls or smacked us, but they were strict and did not laugh much.

The children at the school all had chores to do on the wards. We didn't move around from building to building without asking permission. If we wanted to go to the gym, the laundry, or somewhere else on the grounds, we had to tell the supervisors where we were going. We were never allowed to go outside the PTS boundaries, not on our own.

MY CATHOLIC FAITH

I can't talk about my life without mentioning God. My mother never taught me anything about religion. She never gave me a rosary or showed me how to pray. When I was about five and still living with my mother in Black Diamond, we went to church from time to time. There, I met a Catholic priest called Father Malville who gave me my faith. I always felt at ease when I was in a church. I wasn't scared there, and felt very safe. Even today when I go into a church, I feel very safe and secure. As a girl, I had no hat and went to church with my head uncovered, so Father Malville gave me a Kleenex folded like a flower to put on my head during the service, because in the 1950s and 1960s women had to wear a hat in church. Later, I received my first communion from another priest while I was staying at the Lacombe Home, before I was admitted to the PTS.

At the training school, they held regular weekly masses for the Catholic kids. Boys and girls of all ages went together to the gym where chairs were set up, with the girls sitting on one side and the boys on the other. Father Rowe visited and said mass. There were separate services for Protestants and other religions.

DAY TO DAY

At the PTS, we followed a daily routine. Each day, they woke us up at 6 AM and we washed and dressed before having breakfast at 7 AM. At breakfast, they gave us medications. I remember the little cups they put the pills in, but we weren't told what it was for. Sometimes the medications were given by a needle.

"This communication reports on the use of thioridazine for a wide variety of symptoms in 97 children in a residential school for retarded children. All of these children had failed to respond to one or more phenothiazine compounds. In all cases, even with dosages which produced severe side-effects, there had been no improvement."

L. J. LeVann, Medical Superintendent of the PTS, Red Deer
Alberta Medical Bulletin, 1961, Vol. 26, p. 144.

Only much later in life, during preparation for the trial in 1995, did I learn that I and many other kids in the PTS had been used as guinea pigs for experiments with powerful drugs. Dr. le Vann was trying to find out if there would be fewer problems with bad behavior on the wards on days when we took the drug. The results of his research were published in medical journals, but nobody ever told me about this.

After breakfast, we made our beds, then went to school at 8 AM. They lined us up in the hallway, and we walked two-by-two to school. Then we went back to the wards for lunch. Our meals were cooked in the basement of the administration building where they had a big kitchen, and our food was brought over to us in big steel containers. We had to dish it up from those containers and then wash the dishes afterwards. After lunch, we lined up again and went back to school. At night time, after dinner, there were no snacks; we just got our three meals each day.

If there was any laundry to be done, it was sent to a different area of the institution, where I worked in later years. We never had homework from school like kids today. We got to play until about 7 PM after supper, then bathed and put on our pyjamas. Lights went out at 8 PM when we got into bed. As I got older, I sometimes read under the blanket with a lamp. We weren't supposed to get up and play at night, but we did it anyway! I remember taking shoelaces under my covers and teaching myself how to braid when I was 10 or 11.

THE PUNISHMENT WARD

Like any child, some of the other girls and I did things like talk back, or stomp our feet and yell, "I don't have to clean my room." No child is good all the time, I don't care who you are. But sometimes we were punished just for being sassy. We were supposed to fold our clothes every day and have every drawer checked. Clothes were folded a certain way—socks, undies, pyjamas—everything had to be folded just right. The bed had to be made with proper corners. Everything had to be perfect. I was usually pretty good, but sometimes I just didn't want to do what they asked. I said, "You're not my boss." But of course they were The Boss. Overall, I was punished less often than the other girls, some of whom got punished at lot. In 10 years, I was punished about four times for minor infractions of the rules.

When we were being disciplined, we were sent to one of two different wards that I can remember, Cherry Ward #3, and Maple Ward #4. We girls called them the "punishment wards". If you sassed back to the matron, she'd call for two burly guys to come and take you to the punishment ward. When I first got there, I was put in a little room about 8 feet by 7 feet, made of cement all the way around. I used to call it the "prison room." It was like a cell. There was a tiny window in the door so high up the matrons could see in but I could not see out. There was a rubber mattress on the floor but no bed, the walls were cement, and it was damp and cold. I felt like I was back at home again; being locked in a room and made to sleep on the floor.

I had to stay in the Quiet Room for a few days before being let out and put with the other people who lived in that ward. Those people were adults with serious behavioral problems; they were really disabled or very difficult to control. They were kept there their whole lives. There were no other young people there. It scared the living life out of me. I don't know if the matrons wanted to scare us or just make us work, but I do know I was scared all the time I was in there.

It was so scary to see adults with their faces screwed up all the time, screaming, making weird growling noises like animals. Some rocked back and forth non-stop, while others banged themselves against the walls. Some were strapped into straightjackets all the time because they were violent. We were made to sit very close to those people and feed them with a spoon. We also had to make their beds because they could not make their own. The matrons on the punishment ward were very stern and strict with us, and they expected the beds to be perfect. I remember so well how the bedspreads had rows of red and green trees on them, and how the matrons demanded that we make the beds so that the trees lined up straight across. If they did not line up perfectly, the matron would insist we tear off the bedspread and remake the bed. We often deliberately made the rows of trees crooked so that we could stay out of the ward where the patients were kept during the day. At night we washed the floors.

Sometimes we stayed a couple of days, sometimes a week. The last time I was there, I think they forgot about me, I really do. I was in the ward for quite a while, until I eventually stopped eating. It just got to be too much. I ended up passing out and they let me go back to my regular ward. I was about 13 at the time.

As an adult, I can't eat from tin dishes because of the bad memories of using them in the punishment wards. I had to feed those people a kind of porridge with a spoon from tin dishes. Then I had to eat my own food from a tin dish.

Earl Curr (ward nursing attendant): "If they were misbe-having and say they assaulted another client or outright misbehaved or were destructive or something, then the theory was you used negative reinforcement. The [girls] would be removed to .. Elder Villa, a low-functioning female unit of idiots and low-grade imbeciles. The theory was that you would not want to live like this, so you would want to go back to a better unit and the behavior would improve as a result of it. ... I had worked with lower-functioning clients when I was summer relief there. I didn't particularly enjoy the situation. I was very young and inexperienced at the time and I found it rather traumatic to have a (sic) change an adult's diapers, to see adults that were incontinent and this sort of thing and unable to feed themselves.."

("Muir vs. Alberta", trial transcript, pp. 1056–1060)

SCHOOLING AT THE PTS

The school at the institution was in a separate building behind the Oak ward, and is still there today. It was operated by the PTS, not by the Department of Education. There were six classrooms—two for younger children: Kindergarten and Grade 1. There were separate classrooms for boys. In the classes for older children, there was a wide range of ages in one room. We learned to read and write. Lessons were in the morning and afternoon. I also went to sewing class once a week and cooking once a week. I enjoyed both of them.

In school, we copied stuff from the blackboard onto paper, but I don't remember having books. We didn't have quizzes or tests. The teachers came to school just to teach; some had teaching certificates while others didn't. I didn't know any of them by name. I don't remember any report cards given to parents. I never saw a report card, and there was no promotion from one grade to another. This meant you stayed in one classroom for two or three years. They probably taught us this way because we had been classified as "morons" when admitted to the school. When we were moved to the next classroom, we didn't learn anything different. I didn't get the schooling I should have received while I was in the institution. Grade 5 is all I got.

After finishing Grade 5 at the PTS, we had to work most of the time doing chores at the institution. We weren't paid for any of this work. When I was older, the institution arranged for me to do house-keeping in people's homes in Red Deer. The other girls and I were never paid for doing this work; we were told that the money was given directly to the office and apparently put in trust for us. But I never saw any of this money.

TIME TO PLAY

There were gym classes a few nights a week, too. We played indoor volleyball or badminton in the winter. I really loved both games and was very good at both of them. I loved playing softball in the summer. Sometimes we went into the city of Red Deer to go bowling or swimming. I used to sing at our get-togethers. There was no school at the PTS in the summer. We usually had a trip to Gull Lake where we stayed in cabins for two weeks. We slept in bunk beds and swam in the lake. It was a lot of fun and I loved to be outdoors all day. We decorated our bikes and had races. Prizes were given for the best decorated bike or whoever won the race. I won many times. At our Easter parties, I often won for the best costume. We also had to make something to carry in our hands. For Jesus, I made a cradle out of a shoe, and put a very tiny doll in it. Another time, I made a bible with a rosary on it.

We also had Christmas concerts and dances just like at normal schools. In fact, we had a lot of dances while I was in the institution. At the annual Christmas concert, we all got dressed up and sang as a choir. Parents of many of the kids in the PTS attended along with some people from the Red Deer community. My mother never, ever came to one of those concerts. One year, the popular country and western singer Dicky Damron performed for us. At another Christmas concert, I performed by reciting Little Orphan Annie, all 20 verses of it from memory with no notes! The audience clapped and clapped, which made me feel really proud.

History of the PTS, by Michael Dawe

In 1912-13, the Presbyterian Church built a magnificent four storey brick college on the brow of the East Hill, overlooking the City of Red Deer. The Alberta Ladies College was designed to give "girls in Western Canada and especially girls in rural areas, the opportunity of receiving an education under Christian auspices." ... Unfortunately, right from the start, there were not the financial resources to fulfill the grand dream of providing a high-quality education for young rural women. ... Finally, in the spring of 1916, the college building was sold to the provincial government for $125,000. ...

In 1923, the provincial government decided to turn the newly constructed Home and Training School for Mental Defectives at Oliver, near Edmonton, into a psychiatric hospital. ... The idea of using the old college building in Red Deer as an institution for mentally handicapped children was revived. The facility which had been operating in south Edmonton was closed, and the 50 children who had been living there were transferred to Red Deer in the fall of 1923. In October 1923, the new Provincial Training School (PTS) officially opened.

During its first year of operation, the PTS admitted another 58 children and young adults. They were provided with academic, vocational and personal development training. Initially, admittance was arranged by a family physician or an official with the provincial government. However, as time went on, families were allowed to make direct application for admission on behalf of a family member. ....

By the late 1920s, there was a waiting list of more than 700 for admission to the institution. An addition was made to the college building in 1928 and additional buildings were constructed starting in 1930.

There were many other changes over the years. In 1955, a new institution for the care of adults, named Deerhome, was constructed north of the PTS. In 1965, the PTS was renamed Alberta School Hospital (ASH). Following the release of the Blair Report in 1969, there was a major overhaul and reconstruction of the two institutions in the early 1970s. ASH and Deerhome were amalgamated in 1973 and renamed Michener Centre in 1977 in honour of Governor General Roland Michener.

Published by: Red Deer Advocate, June 11, 2007, p. D7. Article used with permission.

I wasn't allowed to receive visitors at the PTS. It makes me laugh that the school has files listing pages and pages of visitors who came to see me, when in fact I *never once* had visitors while I was there. It turns out that my mother had instructed the school to limit the number of people who could visit me. She authorized just two people, neither of whom was known to me. In other words, she didn't allow me to have visitors at all. This is how much she wanted to keep me hidden. There was one young girl at the PTS whose parents wanted to take me out from time to time to visit their home, but my mother did not allow it.

"The parents of Lellane Scorah wish that only the following people be permitted to visit their child: Mrs. Hanes, Red

Deer. Mrs. Ennis, Wetaskiwin."

Letter from Taylor to PTS Matron, July 13, 1955 (day
after admission)

They allowed us to go home for holidays, but being with my mother
was never a holiday for me. I don't know why she bothered. She didn't
treat me well at all, or show any kind of love towards me, even after I
had been away for months. Other girls at the institution went home
to a nice family and came back happy. For me, being at the PTS was
much better than being at home.

"In November, 1956, Ms Scorah wrote to Dr. le Vann to
explain why Lellani had not yet returned to the Provincial
Training School. That letter contained the following comments:

'Now [Lellani] has a black eye. I was sawing wood with
Harley when I threw the wood to the side of me and it
struck her square in the face. She does not seem to understand to stay out of the way. Heaven only knows when she
really will. I pray soon.'"

(Madame Justice Veit, decision in Muir v Alberta, fact 28)

One time my mother did not want to send me back to the PTS
because I had a black eye that made it look like I had been beaten,

which I had. So she made up a lie. She said I had been hit by a block of wood while she and Harley were sawing wood. In fact, she never sawed wood with Harley, and Harley himself always used an axe, not a saw. I was never hit with a block of wood. My mother punched me in the eye, for some reason I cannot recall.

(**Leilani Muir at trial**) "A: … as long as my mother was home, I didn't want to go home. But I had to—I was scared of her, so I went, whenever she asked to bring me out of there. And if the institution would have had any brains, they would have never let me go back into the environment all the time.

Q: You never told anyone at the institution, did you?

A: No, but couldn't they see when I came back after every visit? Let's put it this way. How blind could a person be?"

(Trial transcript, volume 1; page 257)

When I was 12, I went alone to Saskatchewan by bus for a holiday, changing stations with help from the bus driver. The year was 1956, just after Christmas. My family had moved to Canora, Saskatchewan, because their house in Priddis had burned down and they had relatives in Saskatchewan. My mother was from there. Chris was only eight months old at the time. Uncle Pete lived in Regina and Uncle John was still around. There was some land in Canora that Dad tried to farm, but he just couldn't get into it. I think one of those relatives liked me, because I later discovered that someone had left me some property. I found this out much later. One day, when I was about 24, my mother gave me a blue paper and asked me to sign it. She didn't tell me about the contents of that paper. Later, I learned about a document saying a relative left a farm near Canora to Leilani. It was a quarter section of land, and I had signed it away without knowing. *I never received any money for it, that's for sure.*

Once, when I was visiting my family in Canora, I fell in the well. Although I was 12, I was no bigger than a six year old. My father had just bought a new water pail. He told all of us kids not to let anything happen to it. When I went to get some water from the well, the rope broke. I went to grab the pail, but I fell in headfirst. The well was maybe 60 feet deep, and the surface of the water was about five feet down, so I couldn't reach up and pull myself out. I couldn't swim either, because it was too narrow down there. I was going under for about the third time when Wayne and Uncle John saved me. I don't know how they did it. All I remember is that there was a yellow and black snake crawling around in the well. I hate snakes to this day.

In the summer of 1959, I went home for the holidays to Keewatin, Ontario. One day, my mother asked me who I was sleeping with in the institution. I thought she meant who my roommate was, because there were two to three girls in a room. But this wasn't what she meant at all. What she was really saying was which guys was I sleeping with? I told her, "No one," but she didn't believe me and beat me badly. She just didn't believe me and kept beating me. She made me take all of my clothes off, and she checked between my legs and said, "You did so sleep with someone." I was only 15 years old. Back in 1959, you didn't do things like that at that age.

This type of cruelty was inflicted on me right up until I was about 18 years old, whenever I went home. I was only brought there so there would be someone to clean the house, and someone for everyone to beat on. I cannot remember ever having a happy day at any time when I was home. There, they always called me a moron or retard.

My father Harley was not a mean person, though. He was nice to everyone. He only hit any of us kids twice that I can remember. The first time was when I was home for a holiday in Saskatchewan. My parents were out; I think they went into town. We lived on the farm at the time. While they were gone, one of my brothers took some purple gas and poured it along the side of the road and lit a match to it. We all tried to put it out with our coats and anything else we could get a hold of. We all got a good spanking for it.

The second time my father hit any of us kids, he didn't hit me, he just hit my brother Farley. I was home during the summer of 1961. I was 17. Farley is two years younger than me. I was doing the wash and I went upstairs to get my brothers' dirty laundry. It was noon and I tried not to wake anyone up, but I woke him. He ran down the stairs and hit me in the face as hard as he could. The blood from my nose went everywhere. My father just happened to come home for lunch at that time. He hit my brother back and told him never to hit me ever again. Farley never hit me again after this. Those are the only two times that I can remember my father using his fists on any of us.

Later on, when I was 18 and home for the summer holidays in 1962, my brother Farley and his friend were in a car accident. My brother wasn't hurt, he just had a few bruises. His friend, though, died a few hours later. When we heard about the accident, I said, "Please let Farley be alright." Well, I wish I hadn't said that. My mother turned around and yelled, "I wish it were you! I wish you were dead!" I knew right then and there that there was no love in her heart for me. All I wanted was for someone to show me some love, but it never happened.

From PTS Progress Diary:

"January 1963: Leilani has had good health during the past year and has no illnesses, no accidents. She went home on November 9th, '62. Her weight was then 125 pounds. On returning from home in January of '63, she now weighs 111 pounds. Leilani has frequent home visits during the past year but there has been some question as to whether [they] were beneficial or not while at home."

"August 10, 1963: This girl was readmitted last night. On this occasion and on the previous occasions when she was home for Christmas, she lost 15 pounds in weight. She is thin and perspiring rather a lot."

("Muir vs. Alberta", trial transcript, pp. 93–94)

Holidays are supposed to be happy times when families get together and rich feasts are served. Many people gain weight and then struggle to fit into their clothes. This was never my experience. The PTS records show this well. Evidence of abuse was obvious, but nothing was ever done to stop it.

Letter from Mrs. Hepburn to Dr. le Vann dated November
21, 1962:

"I understand she is mistreated at home and that you're
quite aware of this.

(Muir vs. Alberta, trial transcript, p. 225)

That same summer, my mother said to me that no man would ever
have me or love me as a wife. I didn't know what she was talking about.
I was so naïve about things. When I was older, I realized what she
meant by that remark when I found out that I couldn't have children.

> I am agreeable that sterilization be
> performed on my child *Lillian Marie Acorah*
> if this is deemed advisable by the Provincial
> Eugenics Board.
>
> Signed *Harley G. Acorah*
> Date *July 12/53*
>
> Witness:
> *L.B. Taylor.*

I was brought before the Alberta Eugenics Board on November 22, 1957, at 3:40 in the afternoon. The Eugenics Board was a group of people that decided who should be sterilized as part of the province's Sexual Sterilization Act, a law that ran from 1928 to 1972.

I was told nothing ahead of time. I was 13 years old, and I had just started to have my monthlies. All of the trainees at the institution were presented to the Board at some point. In my case, a nurse just came to the ward one day and told me and a few other children that she was taking us somewhere. She never spoke to us as she walked us to the Administration Building, where we were asked to wait outside the room where the Board was meeting. When it was my turn to go in, I walked in and stood there all by myself. I remember a long table with four people sitting at it. I was presented to them as file number 3280, and the interview lasted only a few minutes. One of the questions the eugenics board members asked me was "how old is a baby when they start walking and talking?" I knew this, of course, because I had a little brother. I said the baby started doing those things at a year old. I thought everyone knew that! They must have thought I was really stupid, and that I didn't know what I was talking about. After I returned to the ward, I never talked to anybody about the hearing or the Board.

I found out years later that Dr. le Vann had called me a 'moron' when I was admitted to the PTS, and that this is why I was sterilized. The Eugenics Board reported that in 1957 my IQ was 64, but we later found out that this was a big mistake. The summary of my case presented to the Eugenics Board by Dr. le Vann actually stated that I was doing well in the PTS school at the time of my hearing.

The Board members who approved my operation were: Dr. John M. MacEachran, a philosopher and Chairman of the Psychology Department at the University of Alberta, Mrs. C.T. Armstrong, Dr. W.R. Fraser, and Dr. R.K. Thompson, who was involved with the genetic counseling program at the University of Alberta. My lawsuit did not name the board members individually because the Sterilization Act maintained those people were innocent. In *my* mind, they were far from innocent and should have been held accountable for their actions. They ruined a lot of lives. Sometimes it took them as little as five minutes to make a decision. That's all our lives were worth—five minutes of their time!

The main goal of the Eugenics Board was to control breeding in the population in order to lower the chances of "feeble-mindedness." They believed that people like me were a menace to society. In Alberta, almost 3,000 people were sterilized under this program, most without their consent. The people on the board were ignorant about our lives and of the permanent damage that they did to us. They didn't treat us like humans, but like cattle on a conveyor belt.

Excerpts from Eugenics Board case #3280 (PTS #1325), November 22, 1957

"DIAGNOSIS: Mental defective Moron

SCHOOL: Since admission to the School, she is doing very well in school, is good in spelling and arithmetic and is a good reader. Lellani is excellent in dramatization and neat in all her work. She is quick tempered and finds it hard to take correction, but is making an effort to become a better loser.

REASON FOR STERILIZATION: Danger of transmission to the progeny of Mental Deficiency or Disability, also incapable of Intelligent parenthood."

One of the board members who approved my sterilization, Dr. MacEachran, was one of the main supporters of the eugenics program in Alberta. He was on the Eugenics Board from the time it was started in 1929 until 1965, the same year I left the institution. Dr. MacEachran retired from academics in 1945 and died in 1971, the year before the Sterilization Act was abolished.

My sterilization operation took place more than a year after my hearing before the Board, on January 19, 1959. It wasn't done at a hospital like most surgeries, but at a small clinic at the PTS. On that day in January, we had our breakfast and made our beds as usual. While I was getting ready for school with the other girls, a nurse came and told me I was not going to school that day. I just said OK and waited in the play area until the nurse came and took me over to the clinic. Like always, I didn't ask why, and she didn't tell me what was happening. She just took me over there. Mindy Fox and two other girls were having their procedures done at the clinic the same day.

There was one thing the nurse said to us that seemed strange, though, and I remember it years later. She said, "Now you can go out with boys and nothing will happen." I didn't understand what this meant because I knew nothing about sex. Two of the girls were talking as if they understood, but I didn't.

Before the surgery, they gave us each a needle with anesthetic while the four of us were together in the room. I remember nothing after that. Afterwards, I threw up and felt really sick, and was so sore from hurting. I asked the nurse why, and she said I had an operation so they could take my appendix out. This explanation was not much help for me, because I did not know what an appendix was or why they wanted to take it out. At the PTS school they never taught us anything about anatomy of the body. All I knew was that I had a big scar across my tummy after the operation, a scar that is still there today.

Excerpts from report by L. J. le Vann of operation on Lellani Marie Scorah

"Diagnosis: Mental Defective - Moron

Physician recommending: Dr. L. J. le Vann, Medical Superintendent, P. T. School

Surgeon: Dr. R. M. Parsons   Anaesthetist: Dr. T. J. Parkinson Assistant: Dr. L. J. le Vann

Anaesthetic: Sodium Pentathol and Ether

Particulars of Operation:

Lower midline incision. Small uterus and ovaries.

Bilateral salpingectomy - oversewn with Chromic #0

Routine Appendectomy with chronic purse string.

Layer closure of abdomen, plain #0 and #000, Chromic #0, Cotton #000.

Convalescence: Good recovery"

We stayed at the clinic for two or three days before going back to the ward. The other three girls were sick too, and recovering from surgery like me. On the ward, I was put to bed in the sick room for about a week because I was throwing up all the time and could not even keep water down. Many years later I learned that a person is supposed to have an empty stomach before major surgery, but we all had a big breakfast before ours. I don't think le Vann really cared what happened to us. After the surgery, nobody ever tried to explain the operation or comfort us. Life on the wards just went on like before.

Mr. Curr (ward nurse) A: "Some of the girls had hysterec-tomies, some had oophorectomies which is simply the removal of the ovaries. Some of the lower-functioning girls had hysterectomies because they were unable to look after themselves during their menstrual cycle or if they had a heavy flow. Some had their fallopian tubes tied, so there were three different procedures that were carried out with the females that were quite different from the male. It was more serious always."

Ms. Anderson (my lawyer) Q: "Mr. Curr, beyond your looking after the children in the ward when they returned, were there any counselling or other services provided for these children after the operation?"

A: "There wouldn't be at that time, no. There was only one psychologist on staff and one social worker. There were no counselors available."

Q: "And did those persons provide, to your knowledge, any

counseling or other supportive services for these children?"

A: "Not that I am aware of, no."

("Muir vs. Alberta", trial transcript, p. 1078–1079)

The surgeon who sterilized me was Dr. R.M. Parsons of Red Deer, assisted by Dr. le Vann. Dr. le Vann was the medical superintendent of the PTS. He set up the special clinic at the PTS where the sterilizations took place, and Dr. Parsons performed most of the operations. I often wonder how Dr. Parsons would have felt if this had happened to one of his family members. Two years after my operation, he was named president of the Canadian Medical Association. He and le Vann died before my trial and never had to answer for their crimes.

At the trial, I learned that on the same day I was admitted to the PTS in 1955, my mother gave permission for them to sterilize me. The first time I saw the actual consent for sterilization document signed "Harley Scorah" was when I was preparing to go to court. Because my stepfather would have never agreed to the operation, my mother forged his signature on the form. I remember once seeing her and my brother practicing writing Harley Scorah's signature. In fact, although he drove the car the day they dropped me off at the PTS, my stepdad didn't even know I was still there years later! My mother told him I was living in Edmonton.

PART THREE

LIFE ON THE OUTSIDE (1965–1986)

Chapter 8: *Leaving the Institution*

I did not leave the PTS because I was *formally* discharged. My mother more or less kidnapped me. On March 9, 1965, when I was 20 years old, she came to the PTS and said she was taking me out for supper. Although she told this to Matron McCrae at the Administration building, she had other plans. When we went to the visiting room to get ready to go, my mom told me she was taking me to her home, and she threatened, "If you don't go with me now, I'll leave you here the rest of your life!" She meant every word; I knew her only too well. So she lied to the matron and lied to the nurse. She didn't take me out to supper that day. I wasn't even able to bring anything with me, just the clothes on my back. All the things I owned were left on the ward. I was to go with her right then or forget it. Thinking at the time that I didn't want to stay at the Provincial Training School for the rest of my life, I went with her. So we took a bus back to her place in Edmonton. As it turned out, my mother just wanted somebody to do the chores at home. Once again, I was her captive.

"Lellani left Oak Villa at 2:45 p.m. with her mother to go out for supper. At this time Mrs. Scorah told Mrs. Allum that she would be taking a bus shortly after 6:00 p.m. to Ponoka .. She stated that she would send Lellani back to Alberta School Hospital via taxi from the Bus Depot. Lellani had not arrived back by 9:30 p.m. and Dr. Le Vann was notified. A phone call was made to the phone number on file to Camrose but the lady answering stated that the Scorah's had not been at this number for approximately 8 months."

Letter from Martin, Night Supervisor to Dr. Le Vann, March 9, 1965

The people in charge of the PTS, especially Dr. le Vann, were upset when my mother did not bring me back from "dinner." The next day, le Vann wrote a strange letter addressed to himself in which he said my kidnapping was a "discharge." He tried to make it look like he was still in control of everything that happened. The PTS shipped all of my belongings to Camrose, and my mother gave my music records to my brothers. Then she sold everything else at auction. I never did get any of my few possessions.

"Please note that Lellani is to be discharged to the care of her mother, against medical advice, effective Tuesday, March 9, 1965."

Letter from Dr. L. J. Le Vann addressed to Dr. L. J. Le Vann, March 10, 1965

Looking back, it's a good thing I went with her that day. If I hadn't, I probably would have never left the PTS. I found out later that my files indicated I wasn't able to look after myself and needed constant supervision. My mother and the institution claimed I could not take care of myself, but I sure could take care of her and the whole family!

My mother was living in an upstairs suite in a house, somewhere along Whyte Avenue. She had just left Harley and was living on welfare. She sometimes worked as a waitress and was dating other men. My brothers Chris and Ron lived with her. Chris was only nine, and she needed someone to look after him while she was out. So I was there to keep house and babysit Chris. A couple of weeks after bringing me home, she bought me a dress so she could show me off to some guy she was trying to get money from.

She kept me there for five months. There was no bed for me, so I slept on the floor. And the beatings continued. There was a laundry room downstairs in the house we lived in, but she didn't allow me to leave the apartment to do laundry. My mother never gave me a penny, because she wanted me to be completely at her mercy. I was never sent to do the shopping because she thought I'd eat everything before I got home.

When I was 21 and still living at the apartment, my mother went out one night with Chris, who was 10 at the time. Two of the girls who lived downstairs in the same house, Minnie and Sara, helped me escape so I wouldn't get beatings anymore. They were living in a basement suite in the same building and were close to my age. I sometimes talked with them when my mother was gone, and they knew what I was going through. The night my mother went out with Chris, the girls came up and knocked on the door. I answered, which I normally wasn't supposed to do. The girls said "We can help you get away if you want." Then they went downstairs and brought me some clothes and money. I left the building and walked down the street.

For the first time in my life, I was on my own. All by myself in the very big city of Edmonton, Alberta, with no one to talk to or go to during this hard time in my life. No job, very little money. After being locked up for most of my life, I didn't know what to do. Every street I entered just seemed to get bigger and bigger. When you don't know anyone and have no family to call your own or a real home, a city can be a very big and lonely place. I didn't even have a pet. How was I going to get along? I was so scared and lonely.

It was dark the evening I left the apartment, so I walked to the Edmonton bus depot. In the depot, I saw my first photo booth. I stepped inside and had my picture taken. I still have the photos that are at the start of this chapter; they show a very lost and fearful looking, thin young woman. I weighed all of 80 pounds after 5 months of near starvation living with my mother. Then, never having been on a city bus, I jumped onto the first one I saw, not knowing where I was going. I told the bus driver I didn't know Edmonton at all but wanted to go to a Catholic church. The bus driver told me that he had to take the bus back to the depot and clean it off first, but he drove me afterward to

Sacred Heart Catholic Church on 96th Street in downtown Edmonton. I went into the church and stayed there for a while. I always felt safe in a church and thought my mom couldn't find me there.

A priest came up to me and asked me questions. Then he brought me over to a shelter that was run by Catholic nuns. At the shelter, I felt completely safe. It was a haven for me. I believe God is with me all the time, and that he keeps me safe and alive. He was certainly with me that night.

That is how I came to live on my own. In the end, this was very lucky for me because my mother tried later on to put me back into the Red Deer Institution for good, as she had promised.

MY FIRST PAY CHEQUE

I stayed at the shelter for a while. Then I rented a small, furnished room with a hotplate and a shared bathroom. The people at the shelter found me a job at the Edmonton General Hospital on the children's ward. The hospital was run by nuns at that time. So, in this way, I stayed in the surroundings of security.

I loved working with children at the hospital, but I couldn't stand to see the little ones suffer. One day, I had just gotten a little one to sleep after I fed him. He couldn't have been asleep more than 15 minutes when the doctor came in to check his leg. The baby had had an operation when it was only three weeks old. Well, of course, he woke the baby. Seeing this baby cry, I became upset with the doctor. I told him he should have waited until the baby was awake. As hard as it was, I know the doctor was only doing his job. A few months later, a little girl died in my arms. She had the biggest smile you ever saw, blond hair, and blue eyes. She was as cute as a button. I took her death very hard, so they asked me to resign.

Then I got a job as a waitress. It was at a little restaurant across from the MacDonald Hotel; I had seen a sign in the window. I had never been a waitress before in my life, but after that first shift my boss said, "Hey, I thought you'd never waitressed before. It looks like you've been doing it for years." It was just a knack I had, meeting people, getting tips. The lady said that I was very fast at my job and clean. She liked that. Little did she know that I had learned to do things fast and very clean the first time, or else my mother would beat me. I went home that night thinking, *I've got to hide this money*, because I still feared my mom would come after me. I hid the money in a sock in a boot. Of course she could have looked in the boot, but this money was mine. I used to earn money babysitting when we lived in Camrose, but she always took it away from me.

I could have lived off my tips and didn't realize at first that I'd get a pay cheque every two weeks! A nun who worked at the General Hospital took me to a bank on Jasper Avenue to open an account and showed me what to do. I made enough to live on, but I did splurge on clothes, something other people take for granted. I spent $30 on a nice outfit. Sometimes I shopped at the Army & Navy store. I had to learn how to do it all on my own.

This was the first money of my own, so I went out and bought stuff I never had before. At a supermarket, I just looked at all the food. I could buy bread and milk for myself, whenever I wanted. At the PTS they fed us apples, oranges and grapefruit for fruit, and sometimes a few special items at Christmas. I didn't even know watermelons or bananas existed! In the store, I saw this big round thing and asked the cashier "What's this thing?" She told me it was a watermelon. I asked if she could cut some and give me a piece to try. So the girl cut off half a slice of watermelon and gave it to me. I loved it so much I bought some and took it home. I was so tiny at the time I could hardly carry it. At home, I cut it in half and started spooning it out.

You see, at 21 I was starting from scratch. In the grocery store, I didn't know what I was buying. I'd only buy a bit because I didn't have a fridge in my housekeeping room. It was overwhelming at first, seeing all of this food. I bought things like canned beans and creamed corn.

With my first pay cheque, I walked to Jasper Avenue and First Street where they had a nice little clothing store. I looked around and the girl asked if she could help me. When I asked "What do you mean help?" she said, "Could I show you something or help you try it on?" and I said, "You mean I can wear those things?" I remember looking around and seeing this red pantsuit. I loved it. I told the girl I didn't want to spend all my money. She said, "Let's see what we can do. Try it on." I did and it fit. Because I was so small, I easily fit into things. She said I could get it. I bought my clothes there for years. The red pantsuit was the first thing I bought after leaving the institution, and I held onto that bag tightly while going back to my place because I was afraid my mom would come and take it away. I remember thinking *I'll have to lock my door because my mom might come into my room and take it all away from me.*

When I got to my room, I was happy, just so happy. Now I get to keep my own clothes! That's such an experience for a young lady. I had enough money to buy clothes because, at my job, I made tip money easily. So every payday, I went out and bought an outfit. It was so nice to have new things that were clean and dry. I used to curl my hair and go out wearing that pantsuit. It was the first time I wore makeup and bought my own lipstick. When I started working at the restaurant, the other girls came in wearing makeup and I asked "What's that you have on your lips and your eyelids?"

The staff sometimes asked me to go out with them after work, but 95 % of the time I went home instead. I felt enormously intimidated when I went out with others. They told stories of when they were in school, dating or going to a prom. I had nothing to say. I was afraid to tell them where I went to school, and I didn't have any dating or prom stories to tell. I felt so stupid.

ALL ALONE IN A BIG WORLD

My former life as my mother's prisoner had been dominated by basic needs for survival. I had been locked up and hidden away from other children and adults for most of my life, so the simplest things taught to preschool and kindergarten children became major challenges for me after leaving the PTS. At the PTS they never taught us basic life skills needed to get along in the outside world. They said we were morons, we would always be morons, and morons could not learn things. On the outside, I had to learn everything very fast.

After years of being an outcast and totally isolated, all I wanted was to fit in, to be worthy of love, friendship, and of being in a good family home. This meant a lot to me, and it still does. My naïveté and ignorance sure did get me into some predicaments. I believed whatever anyone told me.

DATING

Men showed a lot of interest in me. My first date, I can remember well. I only went out with the man the one time, to a movie and for coffee afterward. He was one of the cops who came into the restaurant for coffee all the time. He was in a uniform and I thought he'd be safe. I had my first hot chocolate that night. After that, it was a while before

I went out with anyone again because I still didn't feel safe. It was so hard for me to trust adults, the exceptions being the priests and nuns.

I really didn't know anything about the birds and the bees. I didn't know what it meant when men showed interest in me. I was very naïve and it can be a horrible world. Back then, men could sense the naïveté in me, like a mark. What I haven't told anyone before is that I once met this guy called Philip when I worked at a Smitty's Pancake House on Jasper Avenue. I had been going out with him for a few weeks when he said he knew someone who wanted to take pictures of me. He made it sound so exciting. So, like a fool, I let them take some pictures. It was a terrible mistake. Young girls who have been isolated from the world are very impressionable. I know this first hand. I can see now how young girls are used for another's own gain. Men will tell them they could make them famous and give them a beautiful life. Then, when the men get what they want, they dump the girl, especially the naïve and very innocent girls like I was. So those guys took pictures, and they were nude pictures. I don't know what happened to the photos. I cut off the session, saying "stop," and I cut off the relationship with Phillip. That probably was a phony name anyway.

Whenever I was in a relationship, I was as honest as I could be, but I also had to put bullet-proof glass between my heart and the other person, or anyone I knew for that matter, to protect myself. My family's past and my own past were so wrapped in lies and deceit that it was very hard for me to trust anyone, and I was ashamed to tell anyone about my life. How do you tell someone that your family didn't want anything to do with you? Even today, I feel that honesty is best, but at the same time I keep a protective veil around me to prevent any pain or embarrassment that may come to another person from being with me.

Chapter 9: *A Barren First Marriage*

Standing at a stoplight one day in Edmonton, when I was almost 22 years old, I asked a guy on the street for the location of an address. He told me where it was, then asked if he could buy me a cup of coffee. I said, "No thank you." About six months later, he came into the restaurant where I was working and asked me again if I would have a cup of coffee with him. This time I said, "Yes." This went on for a couple of months, until we started to go together. I really liked his brother and his father. His mother was alright, although she was a little domineering.

I had resumed limited contact with my mother and brothers, who were also living in Edmonton, after about six months of living on my own. They met my new friend and did not like him at all, although I didn't realize it at first. Of course, they did not like anything I said or did.

I didn't know when I married Bill Yuckshyn that I married him out of spite for my mother. Also, I was trying to keep my independence from her. When we divorced a year later, I knew there had not been any love between us whatsoever. Bill was the first man I dated more than once. I wish I knew at the time what I was doing when I married him. Marrying that jerk was the first big mistake that I made in my life. But I was very gullible. He was nice while we dated, and we were married six months later. We were married by a Justice of the Peace. My mother wasn't there at the service, and Bill's family didn't attend either.

ABUSE IN MARRIAGE

From the time we were married until I left him, Bill was cruel to me. He drank heavily. I hid anywhere I could to avoid him. I didn't associate with neighbours and kept to myself, so no one knew what was going on at our place. In those days, people didn't interfere; it was the husband's right to treat his wife as he wished. I became so desperate that I called the police. Our marriage was a living hell, and I don't use that word very often. He was a very mean person, and he was very, very jealous. Of course, I didn't know anything about men, and he was a smooth talker. I believed everything he told me, not knowing any differently. I sure learned fast about men.

One time I had to hide under a table because he came home very drunk. He didn't know I was home. He was mad about something, so he kicked in the T.V. Then he started to smash all of my Dean Martin records. I was so scared. He knew I liked Dean Martin's singing, so he attacked the records. That's how jealous he was. Another time, we were renting a small apartment above a store. There were a few suites there, and I made friends with the people next door to us. They were away one day, so they asked me to feed their cat and check on her kittens. I love animals, and was glad to do it. That turned into one very bad day. I can still see it as if it happened yesterday. Bill was out all night drinking. He came home at about 10:30 AM the next day. I went next door to check on things and couldn't find the cat food, so I closed the door and ran downstairs to the store to get some. While I was at the store, Bill started to kick all the windows out at my friend's place, and he killed all of the kittens. It broke my heart to see those kittens dead at the hands of such a mean person.

The owner of the store had Bill arrested and charged. When the neighbours came home, I told them what Bill had done. I thought they would be mad at me, but they weren't. The owner of the store didn't blame me either. I felt so bad for all of them. That night, all alone in my apartment, I cried so hard. Now I know why I didn't have any animals the whole time I was with him. Those baby kittens didn't even have a chance to live; they were only a few weeks old.

Bill had a terrible temper. What he didn't pawn for booze, he smashed. He was so jealous, even if someone just looked or smiled at me. I don't know how many times the police came to my rescue. Once, we were walking downtown together. As a waitress, you meet a lot of people. This one day, when we were in town, a customer who came in the restaurant where I worked walked by us. He said, "Hello" and smiled at me. Bill was so jealous that he hit me across the face in front of everyone. A cab driver that was going by saw what happened and called the police.

While I was married to Bill, I tried to go back to school and work at the same time. I went to the Northern Alberta Institute of Technology (NAIT) for a while, trying to improve my grade 5 education. I studied Math and English and enjoyed both very much. But I had to quit after six months; I couldn't work and go to school at the same time. At the time I was the only one working and keeping a roof over our heads and food in the house. Bill only worked one month in the whole year we were married.

LEARNING ABOUT THE STERILIZATION

I found out that I couldn't get pregnant while I was married to Bill. It was 1966. I had always had terrible pain and lost a lot of blood whenever I had my monthlies. At one point I was in such pain that I was admitted to the hospital for three days. At the hospital, the doctors wanted to find out why I was hemorrhaging so badly, so they did some tests. They injected me with some dye and found that I had had surgery. After asking me a few questions, the doctor realized I had been in the Provincial Training School. It was common knowledge in the medical community in Alberta in those days that admittance to the PTS almost always meant forced sterilization. I also told him how my mother had once said "No guy will ever marry you." I didn't understand at the time what she meant, but sitting there with the doctor I began to put two and two together. After that, Dr. Hulley, a gynecologist at the University of Alberta Hospital who was working with my family physician, Dr. Goodwin, wrote letters to Dr. le Vann to see if I had been sterilized while I was in the institution.

"This 21 year old girl was a resident at the Training School from the age of ten to twenty-one years. She says that during her period there she was sterilized by operation at the age of fourteen. She is now attending the Out Patient Department here with gynaecological complaints ... She is also accompanied sometimes by her common-law husband and questions are being asked about sterilization. I would be interested to know what operation was performed in order that I may tell Miss Scorah what has happened. At this time she herself is not certain whether she was sterilized. She is going on information she gets from her mother and we understand that the relationship between the girl and her mother is extremely bad."

Dr. G. Hulley to PTS, April 29, 1966

"On 19/1/59 she had a bilateral salpingectomy and appendectomy performed having been passed by the Eugenics Board on the grounds, 'danger of the transmission to the progeny of Mental Deficiency or Disability, also incapable of Intelligent parenthood."

Dr. L. J. Le Vann to Dr. G. Hulley, May 11, 1966

This is how I found out I'd been sterilized. At first it didn't really sink in. I didn't understand what it all meant, and I didn't want to believe what the doctors said. I figured they could find a way to repair me. I didn't pursue it at the time, though, because I didn't really want to have children with my first husband. Later on, I would have given anything in the world to have a child.

I left Bill for good in October of 1967. I found a nice one-bedroom apartment suite to live in. The owners I rented from lived upstairs and were very nice to me. They had the suite fixed up just like a dollhouse! For a while, I was really happy there, until my ex found out where I was living and showed up one day, causing a lot of damage. He literally dumped the fridge over on the floor. I was asked to move out. The landlady was quite nice to me though, and never made me pay for the damages. But she just didn't want my ex-husband coming around again, so I *had* to move.

After that, the staff at the restaurant had to sneak me out the back door whenever my ex came in the restaurant. He used to cause a lot of problems for me. That's why the girls kept watch while I escaped through the back door. He just wouldn't leave me alone. The police eventually got involved and made sure I got home safely. They always came into the restaurant for their coffee breaks, and when I got off work at night and went to catch my bus home, they followed my bus and made sure I arrived home okay. The first time I noticed this was on a cold winter night. I got to my front door and was ready to unlock it when I heard a car horn honk and someone whistled at me. I thought it was just someone being smart, so I ignored them. I unlocked the door and was ready to go in when someone called out my name. I turned around and walked over to a car across the street where two officers were sitting, making sure I got home safely. If I knew where they were today, I would thank them for being so gracious and for watching out for me. It was so good to know that someone cared. This was the very first time in my young life that someone cared about what happened to me, besides God.

It was 1967, I was living on my own after a bad marriage, I had a job and friends, but still never felt safe from my mother. I was afraid that, at any time, she might appear in my life and abuse me in some way. In fact, once when I was returning home to my apartment in Edmonton, I found her leaving my place with a set of my sheets. She'd asked the landlord to let her in, and she went through my stuff. I was so upset! I asked her to give back my sheets, but she ended up taking them with her. I was never safe from my mother.

I moved from Edmonton to Calgary the same day I filed for my divorce. In Calgary, I found a job babysitting four girls and was briefly truly happy for the first time in my life. Three days later, my lawyer phoned me from Edmonton to say he had a court date set for the next day for my divorce. It was a very fast divorce but the court hearing was like a circus sideshow. My mother came to the hearing. It turned out Bill had told her about it and asked her to support him. She didn't like Bill when she first met him, but suddenly she was on his side. I'm sure she took his side because he was mean to me, and she herself couldn't beat me and get away with it anymore. My mother was so verbally abusive toward me in court that my lawyer took me out through the judge's chambers.

Over the years, I eventually lost track of all the friends I had in Edmonton while trying to find myself and find a safe place I could call home.

Chapter 10: *Searching for Home (1968–1978)*

YELLOWKNIFE, 1968

 For the next few years, I moved around quite a bit. In the summer of 1968, I went to work in Yellowknife in the Northwest Territories. I answered an advertisement that I'd seen for a waitressing job at one of the hotels in Yellowknife. I worked a split shift, from 6 PM until 2 AM, and then back to work at 7 AM. After work, all of the girls went swimming in a lake for an hour and then went back to the hotel to get some sleep. The water was ice cold, but it made you feel so good afterwards. I really slept well after the swim.

I was supposed to stay there for six months, but I only stayed for three because it was no place for a single girl who didn't drink or smoke. I just didn't mix with the people who lived and worked there. It was such beautiful country, though. The days were long because it was daylight for 24 hours a day in the summer. The water was so clear and blue you could see the bottom of the lake. You could just stand there and watch the fish jumping.

BACK TO EDMONTON AND CALGARY

After Yellowknife, I returned to Edmonton and then, after a short time, moved back to Calgary. In Calgary, I babysat four girls. I stayed at their place for about eight months but had to leave because the father of those girls kept trying to get me to sleep with him. He kept threatening that, if I didn't sleep with him, he would fire me and find another baby-sitter. I decided to move out. After I left the four girls' home in Calgary, I stayed at the YWCA for a few weeks. Then I moved to Vancouver, British Columbia, in 1970.

VANCOUVER, 1970–1971

I lived in Vancouver for a year, working at a Kentucky Fried Chicken fast food restaurant during the day and at night in a nightclub named the Purple Steer that was owned by the late, great Buddy Knox. Buddy was a country singer known for his hit songs, *Party Doll* and *Hula Love*. I call him my adopted brother. He was the most wonderful person. Even though he was famous, he didn't let it go to his head. He'd mix with everyone. He was just a down-to-earth guy, a really nice person, a very special person to me. Whenever I saw him, he'd give me a big hug and say, "Hi sugar."

Working at Buddy's club, I made at least $200 in tips each night, which was good money. I went home one New Year's Eve with $5,000 in my pocket! The girls always hated me for the great tips I made. "How did you do that?" they'd ask. "It's how you serve your customer," I'd tell them. I was very fast and efficient. I could carry six bowls of soup at one time.

That's how I got back at one of my customers! He used to pinch my back end real hard. I'd wonder, *how can I get even with this guy?* So I was carrying four bowls of soup one day. He had his foot out, so I tripped over it on purpose and dumped all four bowls in his lap. He never pinched me or sat in my section again.

At the Purple Steer, they had topless dancing in the afternoons from noon until 2 p.m. I was off one day, and went there to have something to eat. Because I worked there, I could have lunch without paying for it. I stood at the door talking to someone, while the manager who ran the club for Buddy, Gary Taylor, called the dancers on stage as their turns came up. When he saw me there talking to someone, he called my name. I wasn't expecting him to do this, even though he tried once before but didn't get anywhere. He called my name and said, "This young lady is very pretty and she's not from Vancouver, but a small town in Alberta."

He had all the men there yelling for me to go onstage and dance. This went on for a few minutes. To get Gary off my back and stop it, I realized I was going to have to do something about it. I went up on the stage. I was wearing a light blue jumpsuit. The music was playing and I started to undress. I took everything off, except my panty hose and panties. I was so scared that I ran off the stage and fell over two tables and chairs. I was never so embarrassed in my whole life! I was redder than a beet and shaking like a leaf. I ran into our staff room, and all the girls were mad at Gary for doing this to me. This shows how gullible and naïve I was. I eventually got dressed and went out front, because I couldn't hide in our staff room forever. Gary did feel bad after this and bought me a few drinks. This was the first time I ever drank liquor, and I downed four screwdrivers within a half hour. Gary never did this to me again. Throughout the years, Buddy never told anyone about this, either.

After that incident on stage, I worked at the club for a year. At that time, I only weighed about 95 pounds. I wore fancy baby doll pyjamas that covered everything. At night we wore our own clothes. Gary fired me because they eventually had topless waitresses all the time and I refused to go topless. Even with all that I went through in life, I never did drugs, drank liquor, or smoked.

The next time I saw Buddy Knox was when he was performing in Victoria, BC, in 1987. I went backstage and we talked for two hours. It was so nice to see my wonderful friend again. I met him for the last time in 1994. He has since gone to heaven and sings to God now. He died on February 14, 1999.

QUESNEL

While living in Vancouver, I met a couple in a lounge while listening to music. They saw me sitting alone at a table and the girl asked if they could approach me. Her boyfriend/pimp had sent her over. While we were talking, they asked if I wanted to make some good money. I told them about my waitressing. They said I could make even better money doing what they did. They said I could make good money just talking to guys. They didn't include the sexual aspect. I could earn good money just talking with them and making them happy. Foolishly, I believed them.

They drove me to the town of Quesnel, British Columbia, and booked two different rooms in a hotel. When we arrived, the girl went off, then came back to invite me for a drink in the lounge. I had a Coke because I didn't drink alcohol. They tried hard to get me to take a drink, and they wanted me to meet up with a man right away. They must have been up to no good at that motel before that visit. After I returned to my room alone, the RCMP broke down the door and started chucking my stuff and using the word "prostitution". It was terrifying. I was just opening my suitcase when the door was kicked open. After talking to me for a while, they believed that I didn't know anything. It was a close call. The officers ended up helping me and found me a different room. The couple was charged, and I never saw them again.

I stayed at the hotel in Quesnel for a few days and phoned my mother to tell her where I was, in case of emergency. She then told my ex-husband Bill where I was living. He came to Quesnel and found out where I was staying. I didn't even know he was in town until he climbed into my hotel window! I was terrified! It was summer, so I had my window open a little bit and he climbed right in. I grabbed a blanket and ran to the manager's office in my pyjamas. The RCMP were called in. I don't think I'd be alive today if I hadn't run out of that room.

The next morning, in the judge's chambers at the local courthouse, the judge told the RCMP to put my ex-husband on the next bus out of Quesnel and send him back to Edmonton. Bill was put on a peace bond and had to pay a $200 fine before he was put on the bus. He was told by the judge to never go near me or bother me again, or the next time he wouldn't get off so easily. That was the last time I ever saw Bill. I thank God for that.

I got a job waitressing in Quesnel and decided to rent a house, renting out one of the bedrooms to a young couple to help pay the rent. One night, after I finished work, this young couple and another guy picked me up from work, because I hadn't learned to drive yet. I had to stop at the store to get something for supper. I had a bottle of pop, and I asked one of them in the car to hold it for me while I went in to buy some groceries. I didn't know it at the time, but they put LSD in my pop. At 25 years old, I didn't even know about drugs.

I arrived home and started supper. I didn't know what was happening to me. I was steaming cabbage to make cabbage rolls, and everything started to look weird to me. I looked out the kitchen window, and I swear I saw people dressed in white from head to toe. This stuff did weird things to my brain. My hair was so long at the time I could sit on it. I cut it all off. The three people said that I threw myself against the wall so hard that it was a wonder that I didn't break every bone in my body. They said they didn't know what to do to get me to stop.

The Quesnel RCMP found me along a roadside the next morning. I ended up spending three days in the hospital. I didn't even know my name, or why I was in the hospital. One of the people in the car who did this to me was the person I rented the room to. They each got four months in jail. Apparently I wasn't the only person they did this to. They had done this to another girl before me. I was lucky I came out of it okay, because the other girl never recovered from it.

After that, I lived in Quesnel for a few more months, working as a waitress because I didn't know what else to do. All of my possessions were in the one suitcase I had brought with me.

BACK TO VANCOUVER

Finally, I got myself together and moved back to Vancouver, where I returned to my waitressing job at the Purple Steer on the night shift. There I met a girl who was serving in the navy at Victoria. A group of navy people visiting the club that day told me how nice it was in Victoria, and they said I should move there. So I moved to Victoria in April 1971 and stayed there for 28 years.

VICTORIA, 1971–1997

In Victoria, I waitressed while running a daycare from my home, sometimes looking after six children at one time. I later gave up my waitress work and babysat full-time for a few years. Besides looking after children, I also managed an apartment block until about 1979.

While living in Victoria, I had some contact with my brothers. I visited Wayne at Christmas in 1978 when he was living in Edmonton with his wife and three kids. I saw Chris too, but he didn't have a family at the time. On the same trip I also visited my brother Ron, who had a wife and a young son. Ron beat me badly during that visit and I didn't go back to his place again for several years.

I made some true friends for life while I lived in Victoria, and still stay in touch with some of them. Belle Parker was one of the first people I met when I moved to that city. It was at Easter and I was living in a little housekeeping room in Victoria. Belle lived in a one-bedroom suite with her son, who was nine at the time. I met her in the hall one day. We started talking, she invited me over for supper, and we became the best of friends, even though she was quite a bit older than me. Belle and I had our disputes over the years, but we never stayed mad at each other as some people do. I always helped her out. She was a poor lady and had a very difficult life.

Belle also loved animals. Her animals were her life. I thought I loved animals, but I think she had me beat on that, just a little bit. I bet every time she ate, she only got about three bites of her food, because the animals got the rest of it. The first kitten I got was from her.

Belle had broken up with her husband and was on welfare. I never told her about my past. By the time my trial came, Belle had already been gone for a couple of years. She passed away when I was in Victoria.

It was very sudden. She was rushed to the hospital after having supper one night and died shortly after she arrived.

My friend Belle used to rent her rooms out to help her finances. I rented a room from her when my second husband and I broke up. When she died, the people who were renting from her threw all of her things outside and sent her dog to the S.P.C.A. Her landlady took two cats and put one cat down, while I took two cats—Susy and Buffy. When I had to put them down just before my trial in 1995, they were both 21 years old. It was a very hard thing to do. They had never been in a cage before, so I couldn't put them in one. Susy always had to sleep by me when I was sitting down. Buffy had the bluest eyes and was herself just a ball of fur. I loved them so much. When I put Taffy down, I cried for a week. My neighbours stayed away for a few days because they knew how upset I was. All of my babies are in heaven now and Belle is looking after them for me until we meet again.

In Victoria I also met Sharron and Scott Hewitt and their son Brian. I lived across from them in a mobile home. They helped me out when I first started to learn to drive. Scottie used to do all the work on my car; oil changes or whatever else it needed. Sharron and Scott have stayed true friends.

I loved going to bingo. One of the people I met there was Raulph Powell. Raulph was like the father I never had. I met him and his first wife before she died of cancer. When my marriage broke up and I was staying at a friend's place, I needed to get on my feet and find my own place. I was having a hard time finding a place I could afford on my own, so Raulph and his wife bought me a mobile home to live in. If and when I sold it, I would pay them back, which I did. Raulph got married again and his new wife Julie and I hit it off like we had known each other all our lives.

Chapter 11: *A Second Marriage*

In the building I managed in Victoria, I rented an apartment to a navy man named Darren Muir. The year was 1978. Darren was 10 years younger than me. He lived in the suite just above mine, and had a really big stereo. He turned it on so high that it made everything in my place shake. The bass was so loud it could wake the dead. I went to his place and told him to turn the stereo down. This went on for many months.

I guess he got tired of me telling him to shut the noise down, because he began to come around to my place after he finished work. He even helped with the children I babysat. He really liked Candace and Kelly, the twins. We called Kelly "Macou" because he looked just like him. He had no hair and a little turned up nose. When Kelly was bad, I told him to go to the corner, and he ran on his tippy toes. The kids were so cute, both of them. I loved looking after them, and so did Darren.

One of my cats had kittens. I kept the cats in my bedroom closet with the door open just a little bit so they could get out. One day I heard a squeal coming from my room. I was in the kitchen getting lunch ready for the children. I went into my room and found a little boy I was babysitting, Henry, a very heavy little boy, in the closet sitting on the kittens, with a very big smile on his face. He saw Taffy, the mother, lay with the kittens, so he thought he could sit with them also. I still laugh just thinking about it. I couldn't get upset with him. I have so many fond memories of all the children I babysat over the years.

Looking after other people's children is a wonderful thing, but it doesn't ease the hurt of wanting and not having a child of your own. I felt like such a failure because I couldn't give birth. Lying down with a little one, telling them a story or just cuddling them until they fell asleep, made me hurt so badly because I couldn't have one of my own.

ONE LAST ATTEMPT TO REPAIR THE DAMAGE

In Victoria, before I met Darren, I was very upset about what the sterilization had done to me, and I was in physical pain too. At one point I sought help from a psychiatrist, Dr. McTavish, who interviewed me and discussed all of my problems. He was not optimistic about my chances for becoming a mother.

"I do not see any indication for psychiatric help in this case. It is really remarkable that Ms. Draycott is as well

adjusted as she is when one considers the horror story of
her childhood. That damage done to her self-image and her
reproductive capacity cannot be undone."

Letter from Dr. McTavish, Sept. 8, 1975

I did not give up hope, and I later went to several obstetricians
and gynecologists to see if somehow they could rejoin my tubes. I
wanted a child so badly. Not long after I met Darren in 1978, I asked
Dr. Graham-Marr to perform a surgery to reconnect my tubes, but
afterwards he told me there was not enough tube left to work with.
Again in 1979 I consulted another expert, and on March 13, 1979,
Dr. Rippington performed a laparoscopy to inspect the remains of my
fallopian tubes. He later told me there was no reason for hope.

"A small sub-umbilical incision was was made .. we could
see clearly enough to see that the tube was shortened
on that side and ended abruptly on top of the ovary and
intimately into it. On the left adnexa, there were adhesions, omental, from the previous abdominal incision and
these were stuck onto the left corneal area. .. One had the
impression that the tube had been removed.."

Report on laparoscopy by Dr. Rippington, March 13, 1979

The reports from Graham-Marr and Rippington were sent to
another expert, Dr. Gomel, and he gave his opinion to Dr. Prevost, my

gynecologist. They agreed nothing could be done. They put it bluntly in letters that I read and re-read.

That's when it really hit me. Up until then, I'd been in denial about my sterilization. In 1980, I was seeing Dr. Prevost because I was having a lot of pain with my period. Finally, I told him, "If I can't have children, let's go ahead with surgery so I don't have periods anymore." So, on February 3, 1981, I had a partial hysterectomy to stop the bleeding. Afterwards, my doctor told me that, when he opened me up during the surgery, my insides looked like a slaughterhouse. I just couldn't believe the damage that had been done by the people at the PTS, and that my mother was the cause of all of it.

"The abdomen was opened by means of a low midline infraumbilical incision without difficulty. Upon opening the abdominal cavity, numerous adhesions were present between the omentum and the uterus, small and large bowel and uterus. The right adnexa appeared to be surgically absent, at least no ovary could be found. ... There was a small remnant of the left tube visible and one could palpate what I thought was an ovary but this could not be visualized. With considerable difficulty the uterine fundus was finally exposed after releasing the numerous adhesions.."

Report on hysterectomy by Dr. Prevost, February 3, 1981

SECOND MARRIAGE

While dating and after our marriage, I didn't tell Darren anything about my experiences at the Provincial Training School or about the sterilization. I was still so ashamed of my past. He knew about the pain, the bleeding, and the hysterectomy.

I was 35 when I married for the second time. Our wedding was held on May 2, 1980. We were married by a Justice of the Peace at the courthouse and had a reception at home afterwards. We only invited the people who stood up for us, and kept it small because Darren had to go back to sea the next day. We had a good marriage, a darn good marriage. He was in the navy while I was with him, and he was gone three months at a time. By then, we had moved into the private married quarters at the base, and I was still babysitting. I really liked Darren's family. It felt so good to be in a family that had some closeness to it. I really loved his grandma. It was so wonderful to have someone you could call grandma.

We were very happy for the next four years. Darren often came home and did so much for me. While I was babysitting, he fed the babies, bathed them, and changed their clothes. He even changed the babies' diapers. After the children returned home at night, he vacuumed for me. While I cooked supper for us, he picked up the toys. He enjoyed helping me like this. There are many little things he did for me. I never had to wash one window in the first four years of our marriage. This was a plus. Sometimes he surprised me with flowers too, just because he wanted to.

Things didn't always go so well between us, though. Darren was a heavy drinker and sometimes saw other women. When he wasn't at sea, he sometimes stayed out until the late hours or all night. But I found a way to get even with him. I put the radio on a country station and set the alarm on the radio. It seemed like every morning a song sung by the Oakridge Boys called "Elvira" was playing when the alarm went off. I laughed so hard. He hated that song. That's how you get even with someone. I wasn't hurting anyone and I didn't say anything mean to him. Anyway, I wasn't playing the song, the radio was.

One night Darren didn't come home after work. He went out with the boys and didn't even phone to say he would be late. So I put his supper in the fridge and went to bed really upset with him. When he came home, I had locked him out of the bedroom because I was so mad. I heard something hit the floor, so I went to check on him. When I opened the door, there was a lovely plant on the floor and a Loretta Lynn book, *The Coal Miner's Daughter*. Needless to say, Darren didn't get yelled at for not coming home for supper. He then took me to the movie named after the book. Throughout the whole movie he kept saying, "That's you. That's you." because Loretta Lynn was very naïve and modest. He was right, because I was naïve and very, very modest.

Darren wanted to have a family of his own, but I couldn't conceive. In 1982, we applied to adopt a child. We filled out many forms and were interviewed several times. We both had jobs and could afford to raise a child. Our troubles began when the agency learned that I had been an inmate in the Provincial Training School for Mental Defectives in Alberta. Darren did not know this, but I had to tell the truth to the people at the agency. That was the end of our hopes for adoption. Our application was rejected in 1984.

When the adoption fell through, our marriage started to deteriorate. One day he took off in a car and didn't come back for a week. If the adoption hadn't failed, I strongly believe Darren and I would still be together today. But Darren changed. It was as if he didn't have a wife. He began to be ashamed of me because he thought I was too heavy, which hadn't bothered him before the adoption failed. We also stopped doing things and going places together. He didn't do anything with me or for me anymore.

MORE FAMILY TROUBLES

At home, things with Darren went from bad to worse. Then on August 24, 1984, my brother Ron killed three people. My mother phoned to tell me that Ron had shot his ex-wife, his mother-in-law, and his brother-in-law. His ex-wife had left Saskatchewan and moved with her son to be with her parents in Delta, BC. I didn't believe her at first, so I phoned the police in Vancouver to find out if it was true. I asked if they had someone with my brother's name, and they told me that they had. I visited Ron once while he was in jail. I didn't watch the trial because I didn't want to break down while watching it, and the family didn't want me involved. After it happened, I often thought that if his wife had talked to me first and asked me to stay with her, she would still be alive. I blamed myself for her death, even though I wasn't responsible. Then I really started to fall apart. I was having a breakdown. With everything else that had happened in my life, I just couldn't deal with anything else.

My brother, Ron had such a bad temper. One day while visiting his house in 1978, I was looking in the fridge for something. He hit me with a wooden spoon, so I yelled at him. He said that it was just a joke but hit me again, and I started yelling at him again. That made him so mad that he just kept beating me until I was covered in bruises. If I'd stayed in Edmonton, I would have pressed charges against him, but I returned to Victoria instead, cutting my holidays short. His wife told me later she didn't realize he could be so cruel. I loved her so much. I wish I could have helped her.

Then, my youngest brother, Christian came to stay with Darren and me. I had to stay strong for him, because I'm sure he would have taken his life if I hadn't been there. Christian had come to Victoria to get his life in order and get his head straight. For some reason, he came to be near me. He was having a lot of trouble dealing with what our brother Ron did. They were very close. We both blamed ourselves for Ron's horrible act. At the time, I was so sure I could have prevented this tragic and terrible thing from happening. I realize now that there is no possible way that Chris or I could have prevented it.

I still love my big brother, Ron, no matter what he did, even though he beat me. He's still my brother. That's just the way I am. I love all of my family, even if I don't talk to them or have anything to do with them anymore.

When Christian began to pull his life together during that visit, he met his future wife, Sadie, in Victoria. Just a few days before they were to get married, our mother came to Victoria for the wedding. She stayed at my place because Chris and Sadie didn't have room for her to stay with them. When she came to Victoria, she brought a lot of food with her. All she gave me were two dozen eggs and two bags of homemade sauerkraut. Everything else she gave to Chris and Sadie. I didn't have a job at the time. The second night she was at my place, Chris and Sadie came over to see her. As soon as they sat down, my mother got her purse from the bedroom and gave Chris $250 for their wedding and $50 for his birthday. Christian's birthday was in July, two days after mine. She did this right in front of me. She didn't even bat an eye at me. She didn't give me a dime.

TURNING POINT

That was the last time I saw her alive. I never spoke to her again after Christian's wedding. I never let her hurt me again. The last job I know of my mom doing was cleaning rooms in a retirement home. Three years later, she died. Although I felt really bad that I hadn't spoken with her in those last years, I was just so tired of her hurting me. I had to think of myself. I had finally decided to put my family behind me, for my own sanity.

Life wasn't real for me at that time. I didn't have anyone I could lean on. My husband didn't even speak with me about anything that was going on in his life or mine. First the adoption fell through, and then this thing with my brother killing all those innocent people. I needed someone to talk to, to lean on, and I didn't have anyone. When I really needed Darren, he wasn't there for me. I was all alone. I was at the lowest point in my life. I lost faith in God when everything fell apart in my life, but it didn't last too long, because I found my way back. I'm a strong person in many ways. I know God will help me and be there for me.

After the adoption was rejected, I thought about suing the Alberta Government. It just didn't seem fair to me that the Government and the Eugenics Board could decide on whether or not I could have a family. More than anything, I wanted someone who was responsible to apologize for what had happened to me. I also wanted to find out exactly what had happened to me at the PTS and why. I needed to understand how I ended up this way. I contacted the law firm Dinning Crawford in Victoria, and in 1984 they wrote to the Alberta government to get an official explanation about what had been done. They never did get my files from the institution. I wrote the Alberta Government myself and got nowhere. Eventually I stopped writing and just tried to get on with my life. I decided not to sue at that time.

Darren and I separated in August, 1986. We'd been married six years, four of them happy. He went to live with a woman in BC who had a son who was 19, and that son was robbing him blind. I asked Darren if he wanted to try to get back together. He phoned once, but the message recorder didn't work. I don't know where he is now. He may have read about the lawsuit in the papers, but he never contacted me.

Our divorce was final in May of 1988. Life went on. I started working at the Bay in Victoria, but I was very depressed. My marriage was gone, the adoption had fallen through, my cat Taffy died, then I lost my job and was on social assistance, and I was totally alone. Because of the sterilization, I didn't think I was worthy of anyone, and I even blamed myself for my brother killing those people. I hit rock bottom. I sat down at the lagoon, watching the swans and ducks, and wondering where my life was going. I felt so inadequate because I had trouble mixing with other people. It was like people could see right through me, like they knew how uneducated I was and how stupid I felt. I could never seem to get some of my words out right. I felt really dumb, just like when I was a child. I contacted a lawyer, Lenora Harlton, and talked about a lawsuit, but I was not confident I could win.

One day in December of 1988, I went to see my family doctor. He wrote me some prescriptions. A few hours later, after I picked them up and got home, I thought about committing suicide. Sitting there thinking about everything, I felt hopeless. I laid out all of my pills on a table—an antibiotic, valium, and another prescription—and took a few. Then I felt God at my shoulder, looking over me and telling me the words to the poem that appears after the Preface of this book. It was so serene. God saved my life that day.

I didn't take any more pills. I wrote the poem down instead and then called the Western Community Mental Health Clinic on Sooke Lake Road, close to my trailer. Myra answered the phone. She interviewed me and filled out a Mental Health Services referral form. Under the reason for referral section, she listed "everything, very abused as a child, sterilized at 14 and a half, institutionalized from 10 to 20, brother shot people, feels like ending it."

TWO MEN WHO CARED AND AN IQ
TEST THAT CHANGED MY LIFE

Myra made an appointment for me to come in the next day. That's how I met Dr. Kovacs. I had seen a psychiatrist, Dr. McTavish, once before; he met me for just five minutes and said that there was nothing wrong with me. But Dr. Kovacs told me to talk, cry or whatever I wanted, so I told him everything about my childhood, how my mother beat me, how my brothers did it too because they saw her do it, how my marriage fell apart, how the adoption failed, all the years of being called a retard, everything. He listened. That was the first time that anyone really listened, that someone wanted to hear it all. I was 45 years old and *finally* someone wanted to listen. Why did it take so long?

When I told Dr. Kovacs what had happened to me, his first reaction was to cry. After I told him my story, he said "I've got to introduce you to somebody," and went to get George Kurbatoff, a psychologist, who talked with me for about an hour. Kovacs, Kurbatoff and I sat together to discuss my situation. "I don't usually swear," Dr. Kovacs told me, then added, "You go after those bastards and sue them." When I asked him about the statute of limitations, he said, "Don't worry, you've got a good case." *That was the real start of the lawsuit.* I had been thinking of a lawsuit, and now I had a vision of how good people might see the justice of my case. After that, I went home and cried, because some-body had listened to me and believed what I'd said.

At that point, I started to become optimistic about my life. It was shortly before Christmas in 1988. Things were looking up for the first time in years. I continued to see Kovacs and Kurbatoff for a while after that. I'd go to them whenever I was feeling down.

Kurbatoff later gave me an IQ test in February of 1989, and I scored 87! Even after getting an education designed for a moron at the PTS, I did OK. I was mentally normal! I never should have been in the PTS in the first place.

Jon Faulds speaking to the Judge on the first day of the trial: "My Lady, we expect that you will hear evidence that in the past decade Miss Muir has now twice been tested for her intellectual capacity. The results of those tests are consistent. Miss Muir is not mentally defective. In summary, My Lady, in connection with this branch of the claim, we will submit that the Plaintiff was wrongfully admitted and confined to the Provincial Training School, and Your Ladyship will be asked to consider the level of compensation appropriate for what we submit is ten years of wrongful confinement in an institution, during Miss Muir's formative years."

("Muir vs. Alberta", trial transcript, pp. 18–19)

PART FOUR

EUGENICS ON TRIAL: MUIR VS. ALBERTA

(1986-1996)

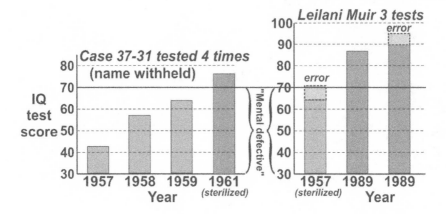

It took me five years to finally decide about starting a lawsuit and then find a law firm that would represent me. After the adoption fell through in 1984, I contacted the PTS in Red Deer, the Alberta Minister of Social Services and the Alberta Ombudsman, but this achieved nothing. I phoned the office of the West Coast Legal Education and Action Fund (LEAF), a woman's legal assistance and advocacy organization, and asked if they would help me. They didn't take my case. The law firm Dinning Crawford had helped me with the adoption application, and they wrote some letters to Alberta, but they never did get the files from the PTS. They told me that chances of winning a lawsuit were not good. Every lawyer I talked with said nothing could be done legally because of the statute of limitations. Because my sterilization had taken place when I was 14 and a half, they felt it had been too long ago for them to build a case. So in 1984 I set aside the idea of taking the Alberta government to court.

The idea of a lawsuit began to take shape in 1988 after my divorce from Darren. This was a very difficult and confusing time in my life, and I was not sure what to do. I phoned Alberta Attorney General Zinger and again the Alberta Ombudsman's office to request my files from the PTS. This got me nowhere. Clearly, I needed help from a lawyer.

While looking through the Victoria phone book at lawyers' names, I found a lawyer named Lenora Harlton of the law firm Price Harlton. I thought a woman lawyer would be more likely to sympathize with my situation. I phoned her and told her my story. Harlton was very interested in my case and began to represent me in October, 1988. She never charged a fee. At last I had the kind of lawyer I really needed. She explained to me how a lawsuit works, and I got the impression this was not going to be easy. In that period, I was not strong. A lawsuit seemed like such a big thing.

Because of her hard work, in 1989 Lenora was successful in getting the PTS to send my files. That was the first time that I saw my files and the lies that were written about me. I was flabbergasted by what I read there and just laughed. They listed me, a tiny thing back then, as wearing size 22 clothes and weighing 122 pounds. I still have a pair of green pants from the institution and the waist is tiny—so tiny that my petite nieces couldn't fit into them. I wore about a size 4 or 6 dress until 1980.

Once the lawsuit got under way, the government was forced to give up documents that it refused to give to me when I asked earlier. They were so confusing. They could not even get my name right! Here is a list of all the different names that appeared in official letters and other documents that were all supposedly about me. Of course, I eventually found out that all those names were wrong anyway. My legal birth certificate says Lellani Marietta Draycott. It took a bunch of good lawyers to get the story straight.

Lellani Scorali	Lellani Mariutto Scorah
Lalonee Scorah	Moira Scorah
Marie Scorah	Lellani Marie Scorah
Sillian Scorah	Lellani Marie Scorali
Lillani Scorah	Lellani Scorer

Harlton wrote to the Alberta government that I had good grounds for a lawsuit, so the government replied that the statute of limitations blocked any legal action. My lawyer was not scared off by this tactic. She said there must be some way. She would have taken on my case, but she didn't have a license to practice law in Alberta, only in British Columbia and Saskatchewan. So she worked hard to find a lawyer in Alberta who would take on my case.

I was still living in Victoria when Lenora Harlton contacted Myra Bielby at Field & Field, a prominent law firm in Edmonton. In May of 1989, Myra Bielby agreed to look at the information Harlton had already collected, and on June 22 she became the first Alberta lawyer to accept my case. One of her first tasks was to address the problem of the statute of limitations. She worked with the Alberta LEAF organization on this and made some strong arguments why that rule did not apply to my case. The legal arguments got really complex, but the outcome was so important for me: The Government of Alberta eventually waived the statute of limitations so my trial could go ahead.

I was *so* relieved to have a law firm that helped me out. In October of 1989, I retained the services of Field & Field on a contingency basis, and the process of suing the Alberta Government began. A contingency fee means that, if we win the lawsuit, the lawyers get a certain percentage of my award from the court. If we lose, they get nothing. It was risky for me and for them too.

On Nov. 6, 1989, Bielby filed the Statement of Claim against the Government. There were three major parts to the claim: I had been wrongfully sterilized, I had been wrongfully confined for 10 years in an institution for mental defectives when I was in fact normal, and I had not been given an adequate education in the PTS. It also stated how much compensation should be paid to me. What I wanted more than anything was to have a child of my own, but the court could not order the impossible. The court could only award money to compensate for the damage done to me.

Bielby was a first rate lawyer, and I guess other people knew that too. Before long, she was appointed as a judge and could no longer represent me. Another lawyer at Field and Field, Chereda Bodner, began working on my case in April, 1991. She was later replaced by Sandra Anderson, who spent hours and hours on my case, working night shifts. The government stalled and put off my trial; they must have known that my lawsuit was the tip of the iceberg. A court date was finally set for 1995. Not long before the trial, an experienced courtroom lawyer at Field and Field, Jon Faulds, joined my team and played a big role during the trial.

GOING TO THE MEDIA

It was so important that the public know about the practices of the Alberta eugenics program that in 1993 I decided to go public with my complaints, even before the trial began. The *Victoria Times-Colonist* and a few other newspapers ran stories about my case.

Headline: Called a 'moron' and sterilized, woman fights back

"Muir's intelligence has been reassessed as normal, if not above ... Muir is marshalling that intelligence, and (her) emotional strength, to sue the province of Alberta.."

Deborah Pearce, Victoria Times-Colonist, June 8, 1993

Many other newspapers and magazines then picked up on the story. At first they were mainly in Western Canada, such as the *Western Report* on June 28, 1993, but as the trial got underway, media from across the country published reports, including the nationally distributed *Globe and Mail.*

THE MANY STEPS IN MY LAWSUIT

After the IQ tests in 1989, I thought the lawsuit should be simple. The government sterilized someone who was mentally normal. They made a big mistake and would have to pay for it. Anybody could see justice was on my side, so I thought. I had no idea how long it would take and how many things would be involved. It was really complicated and seemed to drag on forever. I felt like giving up many times. There was a time when we weren't sure that it would even reach court. At times I just wanted it over with. It was such a long struggle, it really was.

My first discussion about the case with a lawyer was in 1984, and the lawsuit really got going in 1988. The trial was not over until late in 1995 and the judge decided the case in 1996. It took more than seven years to get justice. The Eugenics Board gave my case only 5 min and the operation took less than an hour. So much time and expense was needed to undo some of the damage done to me in a few minutes by careless people.

The public got to know a lot about the trial itself from news coverage, but by far the most time and work went into getting everything ready for the trial.

1. First there was discussion with a lawyer to see if I had a good case.

2. Then I hired a lawyer to start the lawsuit.

3. My lawyers filed a Statement of Claim in the court. I became the Plaintiff.

4. The Statement of Defence was then submitted to the court by lawyers for the Defendant, in this case the Government of Alberta. Their statement argued that what the Eugenics Board and the PTS did was not wrong and no money should be paid to me.

5. Long before the trial began, the main witnesses for the plaintiff (me) and the defendant (the Alberta government) sat through an Examination for Discovery. We were questioned at length under oath by lawyers for the other side.

6. In the discovery of documents, each side revealed to the other all the documents relevant to the case that were in their possession.

Many of them became exhibits at the trial.

7. Each side then assembled a list of witnesses who would testify about facts relevant to the case. They also recruited experts to write reports about issues important for the case.

8. At that point in the process, everything that was likely to be presented to the judge at the trial was known. That is when the Alberta government proposed an out-of-court settlement, but I refused. I wanted the world to know what happened at the PTS.

9. The next step was the trial with several parts described in the next two chapters.

10. There could be an appeal of the judge's decision, but in my case there was none.

EXAMINATIONS FOR DISCOVERY

Lawyers for the government examined me, and then a witness for the government, Dr. Lampard, was questioned by my lawyers. Lampard was the current director of the Michener Centre in Red Deer, the new name given to the old PTS. A formal transcript (a typewritten record of recorded speech) was made of the sessions, to be used as evidence at the trial. I was examined on four separate days: September 18 and 19, 1990; January 10, 1992; and September 3, 1993. Dr. Robert Lampard was examined on September 18 and 19, 1990; June 5, 1991; January 10, 1992; and June 15, 1992. It seemed to go on forever.

My first Examination for Discovery was a very tough time for me. At the Discovery, I met with the government lawyers and Dr. Lampard. He had no involvement with my sterilization or my stay in the PTS. I learned a lot that day. I learned about more lies that were told by my mother, by Dr. le Vann, and by the people at the institution. For one, during the examination I found out that my mother had tried for two years to get me into the PTS; my lawyers had located documents that showed this. At one point, my mother even told the PTS administration that I poisoned our dogs and was a danger to my youngest brother. Our dogs were in fact poisoned by a neighbour lady on the farm down from us in Saskatchewan, because she was mad about something that happened to her turkeys and chickens.

Before they even met me, the government lawyers who came to the Discovery with Lampard must have already made up their minds about me. Outside the examining room, they asked my lawyer: "Why are you bringing a retarded person in for discovery?" They had read in my files that I was diagnosed as mentally retarded with an IQ of 64, and they had apparently based their judgment on this. After the Discovery, I asked Myra Bielby, "What do they think of me now!?"

If my mother had been alive when my lawyers and I retrieved the documents from the institution, I wonder how she could explain the things she wrote to Dr. le Vann, or the lies she told to get me into the institution. I was hurt *very* deeply by what I read in my files; my mother's letters to the institution were written proof of how much she really didn't want me.

TESTS AND MORE TESTS

Before the trial, my lawyers sent me to a number of specialists to have my mental state and intelligence assessed. They wanted to show the court that the PTS had misdiagnosed me as mentally defective, and that I was wrongfully sterilized as a result. To prove this, my lawyers had me travel to Edmonton from Victoria in October of 1989 to have an IQ test done by Peter Lyons, a chartered psychologist, and his supervisor, Dr. Peter Calder. Calder testified later at my trial. He told me I

deserved the Nobel Prize for what I'd been through! I didn't understand a lot of the language the doctors used. When I reviewed the test
results with my lawyers, then I saw how very well I did on the tests.

Calder showed some of my letters written to the government after
I left the PTS to his colleagues in the Department of Educational
Psychology at the University of Alberta, and they said my reasoning
was at the Grade 9 level, while spelling and arithmetic were Grade 4.
He also found a big mistake in how the PTS rated my intelligence in
1957. So even by the bad testing ordered by the PTS, I was never in the
moron range at all! I already knew this, but it sure was nice to see a real
expert take my side.

"On checking the psychologists report of Ms. Muir's intellectual testing, an error in the calculating of the scores was
found; given the reported data her Full Scale IQ should have
been 71 placing her outside the Moron range of intelligence
instead of the reported 64. This error in scoring seemingly
resulted in an inappropriate diagnosis which permitted the
subsequent sterilization."

Dr. Peter Calder report to Myra Bielby, Dec. 28, 1989

Peter Lyons gave me a Wechsler adult IQ test and submitted the
results to Calder who concluded that I was in 1989 a person of normal
intelligence. His report fully supported what Dr. George Kurbatoff told
me in Victoria. In fact, my IQ test score had increased by almost 10
points since February of 1989. Not only that, but on the part of the
test less affected by formal schooling, I was well above average!! Not

only has my intelligence gone up, but so has my self-confidence. Today I wonder what I could have become with a better start in life and a loving, supportive family.

"Her overall IQ was 95 placing her in the average range of intelligence. Her verbal score IQ was 85 (low average range) and reflected to some degree her lack of formal education; her performance IQ of 112 placed her in a high average range within the top third of the general population."

Dr. Peter Calder report to Myra Bielby, Dec. 28, 1989

On January 20, 1993, I returned to Edmonton so that I could have some vocational testing done for the trial. As before, I did well on my tests. The psychologist who tested me, Dr. Roy Irwin Brown, was very nice, and so was the lady who gave me the tests. Dr. Brown was a professor at the University of Calgary in Alberta. He told me he was very happy to get involved in my case against the Crown. He had published a large number of works and was a strong advocate for persons with developmental disabilities.

Then, in February and May of 1995, I met with a psychiatrist, Dr. Paul Edward Copus, who worked with the Capital Health Authority's Child Adolescence Services Association in Edmonton and was a consultant with the Department of Social Services. My lawyers asked him to assess my current mental state, so he questioned me about my background and asked many questions about my life after leaving the PTS. He concluded I did not have any psychiatric disorder.

Oh my gosh, I had to go through all this crap and pain and come to this courtroom just to prove I was sane! I'm not a victim anymore; nobody in the world will make me a victim again. I'm finally standing up for myself, and it's going to be proven when this book gets out there. You can't knock me down anymore. My mother is dead. Nobody can hurt me now the way she did. It's time for me to stand up and be proud! What goes around comes around, I said to myself when I was in the institution.

How did I know that? It came from within and from my belief in God. I thank God all the time for warm sheets and water, for no more beatings and no more being pushed down. If it wasn't for Him, I wouldn't be here today to tell my story. And I wouldn't have friends if it wasn't for God. He put me on this earth and kept me alive for a reason.

The results of Dr. Copus' assessment, along with the IQ tests performed by Kurbatoff and Calder, and Dr. Brown's vocational testing, were the subject of many days of testimony during my trial. All four men were kind enough to take the witness stand and tell the court that I was a competent, capable person of normal intelligence.

LIFE WHILE WAITING

Once the lawyers took charge of my case, they did most of the work. I no longer had to write letters to government officials. The lawyers made appointments for me to see this or that expert doctor. They asked me to locate documents about my time in the PTS and my life on the outside, but I had nothing at all from the PTS or my childhood. Life on the outside left a trail of pay stubs, bank statements, letters, and photographs, but my records were not complete. I never thought the stuff would become part of a public trial, and some things went into the trash when they were a few years old, after my taxes had been paid. Documents and pictures from really bad episodes, such as my first marriage, were destroyed. I did not want things around the house that would keep bringing back bad memories.

I was in regular communication with my lawyers by phone and letter, but there were long periods when all was quiet in Victoria. My life went on as it was before I met Darren. I worked at the Bay and did baby-sitting. My pets needed love and attention, and they got it every day. I had a few friends and played bingo almost every week. At times, the lawsuit did not seem to be going anywhere, such as 1994 when there were no events at all for me to write about. But I knew my lawyers were working very hard behind the scenes, getting all those documents and witnesses ready for the trial. This was the calm before the storm.

It was during the period before the trial that I began to write my book. I called it a journal at first, but it grew and grew.

MY LIFE ON EXHIBIT

Lawyers for both sides located many documents and showed them to each other. Many were later shown in court as 'Exhibits.' They included articles, letters, forms, report cards, tax returns, and photographs. There were also reports prepared for the trial by several expert witnesses. Altogether, there were more than 970 documents that were available to the court as exhibits in my case. About 478 of those were letters, forms or reports specifically about me, while 492 were reports and articles about the general ways that the Eugenics Board and the PTS operated, or how the Sexual Sterilization Act was passed and later repealed. The list at the end of the book gives some of the key events and exhibits in chronological order. Anyone can see from this why I found the whole thing so exhausting and at times confusing.

One of the documents that my lawyers wanted to present was my personal journal—the one that this book was based on - my life story. So my journal was submitted to the court as *Exhibit C093*. Just like when I was admitted to the PTS and given a trainee number, my name was taken away by the system and I was given a number. This is what happens when you go to court; your life becomes an open book for everyone in the world to read or see, and you are no longer a person. That's what happened to me. In the process of taking on the provincial government, I saw my whole life ripped open and laid bare.

PERSISTENCE

I could have given up the struggle at any step along the way, and there would never have been a trial. I got frustrated with the slow pace of the lawsuit but stuck with it. One thing you can say about me: I am very determined, maybe even a little stubborn, and will not let go until the job gets done. The trial exposed my whole life, but it also opened our eyes to how the Eugenics Board and the PTS worked. Before the trial, almost nobody in Alberta or Canada knew what had really happened here. During the trial, we found out that the Eugenics Board and the PTS operated outside the law and violated my human rights. The many facts that were discovered helped to set a precedent and made things much easier for hundreds of other victims of the Eugenics Board who started their own lawsuits after I won mine. I hope my experience will inspire other victims of abuse to fight back and start their own lawsuits. You can win if your cause is just. It will not be easy, but you can win.

HER DAY IN COURT
Leilani Muir, who is suing the provincial government for sterilizing her without her consent at age 14, meets with reporters outside the Edmonton courthouse yesterday. The 50-year-old is asking for $2.5 million. See Page 4.

Instead of flying back and forth from Victoria, I decided to stay in Edmonton during the trial. When I arrived in Edmonton, I had five suitcases with me, mostly clothes, make-up and personal items. As I got off the plane at the Edmonton International Airport, a film crew from the National Film Board of Canada (NFB) was there to film me for a documentary about the case (photo from Edmonton Sun, June 13, 1995, page 1). I stayed at the downtown YWCA in a room with a private bathroom. I was glad for that, because I was there for 41 days. I found it hard to be away from home for such a long time. I missed my dear pets and I don't like living out of suitcases. I couldn't find much to do in Edmonton at nighttime, but sometimes my friend Judy Lytton and I did things together. I saw one show while I was there, *The Bridges of Madison County.*

The trial was supposed to begin on May 29, 1995. Don Thomas of the *Edmonton Journal* wrote an introduction to the case that appeared on page A1 that day, expecting the trial to get going the same day. The front page headline got plenty of attention: "Woman files $2.5M suit over forced sterilization." But the trial didn't get going at all. The trial was put back for two weeks because one of the government lawyers hurt himself skiing. They tried to start it June 5, but everybody could not be ready then, so finally it was set for June 12, 1995. The delay was nerve wracking for me. I was scared from the beginning, and none of the changes helped me to relax. Uncertainty can be very stressful.

Back home in Victoria, I liked to play bingo, but I never felt like playing while I was in Edmonton. I didn't feel well the entire time I was there for the lawsuit, and didn't know what was wrong with me. I thought it was the flu. As soon as I was finished in court each day, I'd go back to my room to sleep. Sometimes I'd just about pass out from the pain; it went straight across my chest. On the tenth day in court, I became ill and had to leave the trial to rest in my hotel. Before the trial, while I was in Victoria, I saw my doctor about the same kind of pain. He said it was just gas pains and told me to take some Maalox. For nine months, I followed his advice.

Back in Victoria after the trial, the pain was so bad that one day I became really sick and almost passed out. My landlady Mona phoned 911. When I got to the hospital, the young doctor in emergency knew right away what was wrong with me: my gall bladder had to be removed! Because it was so critical, they operated right away. The next day, I told my own doctor he had misdiagnosed me. I could have died and he never once said he was sorry that he was wrong. I never talked to that doctor again, and I went back to the first doctor I had when I moved to Victoria.

THE MEDIA LISTENS

About a hundred reporters were waiting outside the courtroom when I arrived on the first day of the trial. They completely surrounded me! I wasn't expecting this and was terrified, there were so many of them, all trying to get a good picture and asking questions. I felt like quitting. What I didn't know that day was that the media's extensive coverage of my case would open the floodgates and get other victims of wrongful sterilization across the world speaking up about their own experiences. A report by Scott Feshcuk about the first day of the trial was published on the front page of one of Canada's national newspapers, the *Globe and Mail*, under the headline: "Woman suing province over forced sterilization. Law allowed government to practice selective breeding." (June 13, 1995) It got people in general talking about the horrifying eugenics program that went on in Canada. People thought things like this only happened in other countries, or during Hitler's time, but almost no one expected to read similar stories about our own country.

THE TRIAL

I was 50 years old when my trial began on June 12, 1995. I was the first witness. On September 14, 1995, the twentieth day in court, the last witness took the stand. Evidence presented at the trial included many documents in binders filed as Exhibits. In November and December of 1995, the lawyers on both sides submitted formal, written arguments to the judge that wrapped up their cases based on trial evidence. Madame Justice Veit delivered her *Decision and Reasons for Judgment* on January 25, 1996.

THE LEGAL TEAMS

My lawsuit was a big and expensive production. The Alberta Government assembled a large legal team and tried very hard to win. I met so many government lawyers throughout the lawsuit that I could hardly keep track. At the trial, they included Mr. D. H. Lewis, Mr. W.C. Olthuis, Mr. R.F. Taylor, and Ms. L. Neudorf. In court, my team was made up of Ms. S.M. (Sandra) Anderson and Mr. P.J. (Jon) Faulds. Sandra did most of the research before the trial, looking up old documents, locating witnesses, and pulling everything together. In court, she played a large role in questioning the witnesses on both sides. Jon Faulds was a more experienced lawyer who joined Sandra not long before the trial and questioned some of the witnesses. Jon also engaged in many courtroom discussions with the judge and government lawyers.

THE JUDGE

There couldn't have been a better judge for my case. Madame Justice Joanne Veit kept a close eye on the courtroom and didn't let anyone get away with anything. If anyone misbehaved in court, out they went. At one point she even gave Dr. Lampard hell! During the trial, he kept going over to the government lawyers' desk. You see, once the trial started, no one was allowed to approach the area where the lawyers sat because all the files were kept there. Justice Veit finally told him enough was enough, and asked him to stay away from the lawyers' desk.

While I was on the stand, a government lawyer asked me to read through some papers from my PTS file, documents that showed my behavior as being sassy. To me, I was just doing things a normal child did. I laughed and said, "Can't you find anything good about me in these files?" The lawyer started to say something, but Judge Veit put her hand up and stopped him short. She said, "I'm not sure sassy for a girl is necessarily a bad thing. Sassiness is good for us women." She had the whole courtroom laughing! Her comment was even quoted in a national newspaper. That's when I started to feel I was going to win my case against the government.

THE WITNESSES

Including myself, there were 17 witnesses in all—nine testified for my side, the other eight testified for the government. Some of the witnesses spent more than a day standing at the front of the courtroom and being questioned. The table shows the order of testimony and the amount of time each person was on the stand. It also shows the pages in the official transcript of the trial where the testimony is given. Details of some of the testimony are provided in the next chapter.

I was questioned for two and one half days, and that part of the trial took up more than three hundred typed pages, which is longer than the manuscript for this book! My words at the trial would not make a very good book, because many of the questions by the government lawyers were pretty dumb. Sometimes it seemed like they just wanted to hear themselves talk. At other times, I think they were trying to get me confused and make me contradict myself or change my story. Sometimes they succeeded and made it look like my memory of events early in my life was not very good. The judge even commented on this. Luckily, there was plenty of evidence in my PTS files and other documents to show how I had been abused and mistreated by my mother and the PTS. It wasn't just my word against Dr. Lampard's.

WITNESSES AT THE TRIAL: DATES (IN 1995),
PAGES IN OFFICIAL TRANSCRIPT,

Date	Pages	Morning	Afternoon
June 12	1–114	Leilani Muir	Muir
June 13	115–242	Muir	Muir
June 14	243–379	Muir	Kurbatoff
June 15	380–549	Kurbatoff; R. Brown	R. Brown
June 16	550–713	R. Brown	R. Brown
June 19	714–871	Calder	Calder
June 20	872–1021	Calder; Robertson	Calder
June 21	1022–1212	Curr	Copus
June 22	1213–1294	C. Brown	C. Brown
June 23	1295–1427	C. Brown; Robertson	Robertson
June 26	1428–1553	Robertson	Robertson
June 27	1554–1650	Read-in: Lampard	G. Smith
June 28	1651–1797	G. Smith; Peace; Thompson	Liddell
June 29	1798–1926	Thompson	Thompson
June 30	1927–2010	Thompson	B. Smith
Sept. 8	2011–2143	Hepburn; Paton	Keegan
Sept. 11	2144–2267	Keegan	Keegan
Sept. 12	2268–2399	Keegan	Keegan
Sept. 13	2400–2452	Keegan	Keegan
Sept. 14	2453–2537	Keegan	Read-in: Muir

One witness for the government made me particularly angry: Dr. Margaret Thompson, who served on the Eugenics Board from 1960 to 1962. She believed that genetics was the "overwhelming factor" in intelligence. While on the board, she authorized and gave instructions for the castration of Down Syndrome boys and men at the PTS, to get tissue samples for research she was doing with Dr. le Vann. There was absolutely no need to put them through that, because Down Syndrome boys are sterile. Dr. Thompson later left Alberta to conduct research in genetics at Bar Harbor, Maine, USA, in 1962, then went on to be a professor at the University of Toronto in Ontario. To me, what she and le Vann did seemed like cruelty to those captive boys. On the stand, Dr. Thompson did not even seem ashamed of her conduct. In 1995, more than 30 years after the castrations, she was still defending her actions and saying no harm was done to the boys because they couldn't father a child anyway.

FRIENDS AND SUPPORTERS

On the first day of the trial, I sat on the hard wooden bench behind my lawyers. On the second day, a court reporter brought me a comfortable chair, a jug of ice water, and a box of Kleenex, and continued to do this every morning and afternoon of the trial. Being treated like a human being by that young woman made the courtroom experience so much easier for me.

Two people who also grew up in the PTS came to my trial every day. Judy Lytton, for one, was with me on both PTS wards. It was so good to meet her again 30 years later, because of the trial, and we have become close friends. Today we attend conferences on eugenics together, and we belong to a group researching the history of eugenics in Alberta. Another person Judy and I knew as a child came to the trial from Calgary. John stayed in Edmonton the entire last week of my trial. He and Judy were a great support for me, because they went through the same thing I did. I also met another girl I grew up with in the PTS, Doreen. She had a memory like a steel trap and remembered everything that happened while she was there. It was good to see the girls I knew as a child and as a teenager. They're true friends who really understand what I went through.

At the start of the trial, the courtroom was almost full. Dozens of reporters were present, writing down notes for their articles. The trial had received much attention in the media, especially in Edmonton, so many in the audience were local people who got interested in the case. As the case dragged on and on, there were fewer and fewer people watching the show. On the very last day of testimony when a witness for the government (Keegan) appeared for the fourth day in a row, there were only three people in the audience: Judy Lytton, John, and Doug Wahlsten, a professor at the University of Alberta who taught a course about genetics and intelligence.

AN OMEN DURING THE TRIAL

Going to trial was so hard and nerve-wracking, and there were days I didn't think I would get through it; I just wanted to get it all over with. When I was on the stand, I had my rosary in my hands at all times. It was a light blue colour. One day during my trial, I went back to the YWCA and lay down because I wasn't feeling well. I had my rosary in my hand when I went to sleep, because I was praying. When I awoke, it was no longer blue; it was white. I believe in God very much. That day I knew I was going to win my case. Miracles do happen.

POSTSCRIPT: MEDIA ACCESS TO EXHIBITS

Some members of the media wanted access to the trial Exhibits for their articles. In an unusual move, the *Edmonton Journal* even hired a lawyer to argue their case. At that time, I didn't want the media to turn the details of my personal life into news, so I asked the judge to keep my journal—referred to during the trial as Exhibit C093—under lock and key. In the end, the media was allowed to make copies of all exhibits except for my journal. And any names of PTS students other than me were blacked out, to protect their identities, because many of the former trainees did not want their families or friends to know they had spent time at an institution for "mental defectives."

THE TRIAL TRANSCRIPTS SHOW THE DISCUSSION ABOUT MEDIA ACCESS.

June 14, 1995. Justice Veit: *Now I received another communication from the media. This doesn't often happen to me, two—two in one trial so far. ... in terms of openness of the process, but also it's an interesting comment, let me just read it out:*

> *"Re media request to view and videotape select court exhibits. It occurs to me that in the ongoing Bernardo trial in Toronto the media have been granted access to videotapes and photographs that have also been entered as exhibits. I vividly remember a front page newspaper photo of Karla Homolka with black eyes, and seeing wedding videos, plus a home video shot by Bernardo the night Tammy died, on CTV, seeing on CTV those videos. I'm not sure if there can be any parallel drawn to what we request in this suit or not, but thank you for allowing me to draw it to your attention."*

This is from a reporter from CFRN TV who makes a very good point, and indeed I say or note for that person's benefit ... that indeed this is an issue that—that I've talked to the lawyers about ... we've had a group of new decisions in the Bernardo trial, both at the trial level and beyond, which although not ... arising in the same way as the issues in this case, may still be of assistance to us as we explore the values that we're dealing with and the way in which we can best meet our objective to support those values

("Muir vs. Alberta", trial transcript, pp. 378–379)

June 16, 1995. Justice Veit: *Sorry to keep you waiting. Please sit down. There are a few other issues about access to exhibits that I hadn't focused my mind on when we'd spoken about this issue previously, and one of the issues which is potentially important in any case where the media is wanting access to the exhibits and may reproduce them, and a feature which I didn't mention yesterday, Mr. Kozak, in this particular trial is that there has been evidence from the Plaintiff to the effect that she is wishing to write a book, perhaps in collaboration, about her life experience. And indeed one of the exhibits that's been entered and referred to is ... let's say a draft or an outline as I understand it of what that book might contain...*

One of the reporters, Ms. Johnson from CFRN TV, talked about the Karla Homolka picture, and then said that maybe the black eye photograph had not been obtained through court sources but through other sources.

... Anyway, I should have asked you first, are you here to make submissions or not?

Mr. Kozak: *Yes, indeed I am My Lady. I'm appearing on behalf of the Edmonton Journal and the Canadian Broadcasting Corporation for the purpose of applying for access to the documents and photographs that have been marked as exhibits in these proceedings.*

(Mr. Kozak went on to cite four cases, including some criminal trials of great notoriety, where the media had been granted access to exhibit material.)

("Muir vs. Alberta", trial transcript, pp. 550–555)

Justice Veit: *All right. While we're talking about that, it has struck me that, for example, on the one hand Ms. Muir doesn't want some screen writer to come along and grab that and say huh, this sounds like a good movie, and so now because it's an exhibit, this—I'm taking this, and I'm going to reshape this and add dialogue and...*

("Muir vs. Alberta", trial transcript, p. 570)

Justice Veit: *Okay. Thank you all very much. This is an unusual case in terms of the process because normally the clerk would be able to look to the AG's Department for legal advice, but in this case, the Department is itself a litigant.*

("Muir vs. Alberta", trial transcript, p. 577)

Justice Veit: *So all I can do now is to give my decision on the issue of access to exhibits in this trial... Exhibit C093 can be accessed, but not reproduced.*

("Muir vs. Alberta", trial transcript, p. 656)

Thankfully, the media slowed down after that, because the court didn't allow cameras to film the proceedings inside the courtroom. I remember one reporter who came to the trial every day, Don Thomas, who worked for the *Edmonton Journal*. His newspaper ran a daily feature of his articles during my trial entitled "The Muir File."

Chapter 14: *Twenty Days of Testimony*

In this chapter, long quotes from the transcripts (photo at left) are shown in italics rather than in boxes. Here I just want to touch on some of the highlights of the trial. So much of it was tedious and boring. The witnesses remained calm. Nobody shouted. Nobody wept, except me on one occasion. But there were a few surprises, and the media usually found things worth writing about each day.

DAY ONE (JUNE 12, 1995) THE GOVERNMENT ADMITS WRONGFUL STERILIZATION

The trial began with opening remarks given by the Crown (Alberta Government) lawyer, my lawyer, and the judge. The Crown lawyer stunned the courtroom when he admitted to wrongdoing on the part of the Alberta Government.

Mr. Lewis: *My Lady, given the facts of this case, the Crown would first like to make a statement with respect to an admission of liability. The Crown acknowledges that the Plaintiff is entitled to damages with respect to the claim of sterilization. The Crown states that in the present case adequate testing was not undertaken with respect to the decision as to whether the Plaintiff should be sterilized. This admission is made only with respect to this case and with respect to the sterilization alone. The sterilization was an irreversible medical decision.*

However, this admission should not be construed as dealing with the testing generally in terms of the Plaintiff's admission to PTS, continued stay at PTS, and the development of an education and training program while at PTS. With respect to these matters, the Crown states that the testing was appropriate and clearly met the standard of care in Alberta at the relevant time. Thus, the Crown recognizes liability with respect to the Plaintiff in light of these peculiar facts, only with respect to the sterilization.

("Muir vs. Alberta", trial transcript, pp. 1–2)

I really wasn't expecting the government to admit from the start to being wrong for sterilizing me, but I was so glad, because it made my case a lot easier. At least they'd admitted they'd been wrong about something! An admission of guilt was what I wanted more than anything when filing my lawsuit. The media were excited to hear it too, because it was all over the news the next day.

DAYS ONE TO THREE (JUNE 12–14) I FINALLY GET TO TELL MY STORY IN COURT

After both lawyers' opening statements were made, I spent two and a half days on the stand. My lawyers, Sandra and Jon, were the first to question me, followed by Mr. Lewis, the Crown lawyer. That was one scary time for me. I was the first person to testify. I'd never gone through something so big and important. It was hard, but I knew I had to do it for myself and for others who had been wrongfully sterilized. Others who have testified in court know what I mean about being on the witness stand—your nerves are on edge.

On the second day of the trial, Mr. Lewis questioned me about my name, my age, where I lived, where I worked, if I lived with someone or alone, if I had animals... they were such stupid questions. Then he asked me about attending schools and such, things that were right there in the documents, about events that happened when I was between two and six years of age, and about my parents. This went on for two days. The government lawyers hammered me with questions, sometimes very confusing ones, trying to establish that I wasn't a reliable witness, I was of below average intelligence, and I was known for throwing temper tantrums in the PTS and for other bad behaviours. At one point, I lost my patience and told them to just get on with their crap!

Mr. Lewis Q: When did you start to walk?

Leilani Muir A: At any normal age that a child does, at about 1 or whatever.

Q: How do you know you started to walk when you were one year old?

A: Because my older brothers told me so and they should know.

Q: All right. So you're relying on your older brothers then?

A: Yes.

Q: You have no personal recollection of starting to walk?

A: No. But I was cooking breakfast and everything at 6 so I had to be normal [at age 1], too.

Q: I understand that you also disagree with line 13 of the developmental history which states that you had staring spells; is that correct?

A: No, I did not have staring spells.

Q: All right.

A: Staring in the corner since I spent 98 percent of my time in the corner.

Q: Do you also disagree with line 15 which indicates that you were four years old when you started to talk?

A: Yes, I disagree with that.

Q: When did you start to talk?

A: Before I was two.

Q: How do you know that?

A: My brother's—my older brothers told me that.

Q: Which brothers particularly told you that?

A: [Ron and Wayne]

Q: Ms. Muir, at the top of page 2, there's a reference on line 16 that "her speech is blurred at times". Was your speech blurred at times?

A: It is now to this day.

Q: So you would agree with that, then?

A: No, no.

Q: All right.

A: I disagree with all of it. Anything you're asking here, I disagree with. Like how can you ask me something about when I was a small child. Nobody is going to remember this stuff, come on. I don't care who you are, even a genius.

("Muir vs. Alberta", trial transcript, p. 192–193)

DAYS THREE TO NINE (JUNE 14-16, 19-22) SPOTLIGHT ON MY INTELLIGENCE

Several results of IQ tests given before the start of the trial have already been mentioned in Chapter 12. At the trial, government lawyers tried to find things wrong with the testing and the way results were interpreted. All the witnesses concluded I was mentally normal. I already knew this by 1995, but it helped to have real experts back me up.

George Nicholas Kurbatoff was a clinical psychologist employed by the BC government who received an M.A. degree from the University of Washington. He was licensed by the BC College of Psychologists to give IQ tests, and he was the first specialist outside the PTS to test my IQ. In 1989 he gave me the Wechsler Adult Intelligence Scale (WAIS) test. He told the court my IQ of 87 was in the normal range, a little below the average score of 100 for normal people. On the parts of the test involving mainly verbal abilities, the part most sensitive to schooling, my IQ was 85, and on the "performance" parts it was 92. Kurbatoff told the court: *"Well, I—I was surprised—based on her history, I was—I was quite surprised that she had scored as high as she did. I can't—and*

I can't account for why she scored as high as she did, except through some growth." (trial transcript, pp. 333–334) He said that his interview with me showed I was not mentally defective. The government lawyers then questioned Kurbatoff in nitpicking detail for an entire day, but they could not find anything wrong with his test or my scores. His testimony in the transcripts takes up 96 pages, but he only told the court four facts.

Dr. Roy Irwin Brown taught at the University of Calgary in Alberta. He was a member of a number of international organizations studying mental deficiency and developmental delays, including the International Association for the Scientific Study of Mental Deficiency.

Jon Faulds Q: And looking at that section of the physician's certificate and the—what has been filled out there, can you tell us, Dr. Roy Brown, whether, in your opinion, that constitutes an adequate and proper basis for a finding of mental deficiency?

Dr. Roy Brown A: No, there is—obviously by the omission of an intelligence test from this record, we don't have the definitive evidence that, in fact, we're dealing with a child who had mental retardation.

Q: Looking at the—what has been filled out there, under appearance and conversation, is there anything there to suggest mental deficiency?

A: No, on the contrary. We have, I think, a clear description of a normal child.

("Muir vs. Alberta", trial transcript, p. 448)

Jon Faulds Q: And if you look down at the bottom of that form, you'll notice that there appeared to be a number of lines which have initials beside them. Do you see that?

Dr. Roy Brown A: Yes.

Q: Okay. And what does this [blank] form appear to contemplate be filled in there?

A: That there would be a number of measures of intelligence over a period of time.

Q: And is that consistent with your description of what the state of knowledge was in the 1950s?

A: Yes. Presumably, this form had been [prepared] in this way as a standard document because people realized that was relevant and important.

Q: And now, the form that we have relating to Leilani Muir, does that, in fact, disclose repeated testing of her intelligence over the years?

A: No, it does not. It provides only one assessment in 1957.

Q: In your view, is that up to the standards of the day for the assessment and treatment of individuals in such an institution?

A: No, it is not.

("Muir vs. Alberta", trial transcript, p. 455–456)

Dr. Peter Calder was a Professor in the Department of Educational Psychology at the University of Alberta. He was very experienced with psychological tests and had supervised hundreds of assessments. He had an M.A. degree in counseling from the State University of New York and a Ph.D. from Indiana University. He supervised the IQ testing that was done on me in Edmonton in 1989 by Peter Lyons. At the trial he told the court that he had found a mistake in the original test scoring by Lyons, and he said my WAIS IQ was 90, with the performance IQ of 101 being higher than the verbal score of 84. He told the court that this was a common pattern for people without much formal education. The results were similar to what Kurbatoff had found, although my performance score seemed to be going up.

Dr. Peter Calder: At the end of the testing ... I asked Dr. Lyons, first of all 'How did she perform?' And he said, 'Boy, she was really fast. She really got the things, really performed.' ...

Calder: I met Miss Muir, I think we talked for about, oh, upwards of three quarters of an hour. Probably she would have perceived it as a friendly conversation, but I am asking for pointed, you know, some little pointed questions and looking for clues. My—my assessment was this was an individual who was far from retarded.

("Muir vs. Alberta", trial transcript, p. 693–694)

Mr. Olthuis for the government Q: Sir, you told us the other day that you were conscious of the role of bias in your opinion and I believe you suggested that this lady deserved a Nobel prize, or at least that thought had gone through your mind?

Dr. Calder A: That's right.

Q: And you were trying to be careful not to let your heart get in the way of the facts, is that right?

A: That's right.

Q: And you were quite complementary of Miss Muir in terms of what she had accomplished and what she had done on her own?

A: That's right.

("Muir vs. Alberta", trial transcript, p. 1013–1014)

John Earle Curr worked at the PTS for 37 years, beginning as an attendant and advancing to mental deficiency nurse and then nursing instructor when it became the Michener Centre. He had a diploma in nursing from Red Deer College. Curr claims to have never met me when I was living at the institution. I think he worked mainly on the boys' wards.

Ms. Anderson Q: This is a ward admission record for Ms. Muir... Can I draw your attention to the third line from the top of the information there that says mental condition?

Mr. Curr... A: Yes. It says 'seems intelligent, moron'. That, in my opinion, would not be, that should not be written that way. That was not what was intended by that. If I was a charge nurse, I would not accept that ward admission record going in like that.

("Muir vs. Alberta", trial transcript, p. 1037)

Mr. Curr A: it [the admission record] says under scars and location, a number of very small scars on body, two scars on right knee, two scars on left knee and then on the right, scar under chin.

Q: Now what, if anything, would tell you that?

A: Well, if that child was not an epileptic child and had fallen and gotten these scars, I would be concerned either this child had been abused or that this child was very prone to accidents and it would need a lot of watching, a lot of supervision.

("Muir vs. Alberta", trial transcript, p. 1040)

Dr. Paul Edward Copus was a psychiatrist working at the Capital Health Authority in Edmonton, and was a Clinical Associate Professor at the University of Alberta. He had an M.D. degree from the University of Cambridge. In 1995, he interviewed me several times for more than five hours about my current life and background, and he concluded that I had no psychiatric or personality disorders.

Dr. Copus: The advantage of this (institutional) sort of setting is that the individual is protected and some conditions can be helped, but the disadvantage is that the regimentation and the nature of the institution are usually such that personal—close personal contact is impossible and that particularly for children the normal function of attachment and learning the skills of intimate relationships are not available to them. The result is that when an individual is discharged from an institution they often have considerable difficulty in coping with outside life or if they don't have that sort of difficulty, then they still have difficulty in forming close attachments to other people. One of the characteristics among children is that they are very friendly but in an overly friendly and indiscriminate way so they are very capable of making lots of superficial attachments but later in life when they have a need to form closer attachments, this is very difficult for them and may cause them real difficulties and real pain in their adult lives.

Jon Faulds Q: But can you say why you used that term in relation to your report concerning Ms. Muir?

A: Well, she was in an institution for the subnormal for the entire period of her adolescence and early adult life and I would—I made an association between some of the difficulties that she described in her interpersonal relationships with the experience that she had had at that time.

("Muir vs. Alberta", trial transcript, pp. 1161–1162)

Ms. Cara Lane Brown had an M.A. degree in economics from the University of Calgary and was employed by Economica as a consultant on calculating damages in lawsuits. She tried to estimate how much income from earnings as an adult I must have lost because of my poor education in the PTS. In the end, the court did not use those figures to compute damages.

So the witnesses for my case told the judge that there was evidence of physical abuse at home and this might have affected my behavior. Living in the institution might have had a bad effect too. Despite those things, I did OK on IQ tests, and experts who interviewed me all said I was mentally normal. Today I can only wonder what I might have achieved if I had been raised in a good home by loving parents. I sincerely hope that children today who live in good homes will realize how lucky they are.

DAYS 10 AND 11 (JUNE 23, 26) AN EXPERT REVIEWS
EUGENICS BOARD FILES

Dr. Gerald Robertson was a Professor of Law at the University of Alberta who specialized in mental health law. For the trial, he reviewed patient files and minutes from Eugenics Board meetings, and he prepared a long report on the history of eugenic sterilization in Alberta. He never met with me, and his report said nothing about me. One fact he discovered from the minutes was that, on average, the Eugenics Board devoted about five minutes to each case that was presented to it. Very often they just stated "passed clear" or "the usual" and said nothing specific about a person. From my file, it appears that they had no real discussion or disagreements about me. All four of the Eugenics Board members thought I was a moron and should be sterilized. Nobody at the hearing represented my interests.

DAY 12 (JUNE 27, 1995) DR. LAMPARD'S EXAMINATION FOR DISCOVERY READ IN COURT

Dr. John Robert Lampard received his doctorate of medicine from the University of Alberta. He succeeded le Vann in 1983 as Medical Director of the Provincial Training School in Red Deer. Dr. Lampard was examined for discovery in 1990 by my first lawyer, Myra Bielby and again in 1991 and 1992. Although he didn't testify in court, his evidence about the PTS was read into the court record during the trial. Dr. Lampard did not know me and had nothing to do with my stay at the PTS. As Director of the PTS during the lawsuit, however, he had access to many documents that told about things that involved me.

During his Examination for Discovery, there were some questions he could not answer right then and there, so my lawyer asked him to make an "undertaking" to find out the answers. Later (June 5, 1991) he submitted written answers to those questions. Some of his answers tell important things about my experience, things that I did not know or could not remember.

Undertaking #5: November 14, 1952 - Letter from Provincial Guidance Clinic to Dr. le Vann. "The above named eight year old girl … is not reported as a school problem."

November 15, 1953. … Dr. Hanley (the consulting Psychiatrist) indicated that "he was not sure of the diagnosis, but thought that there was an emotional involvement rather than a primary mental deficiency."

October 4, 1963 - Welfare Officer (Dorothy Clapson) investigated the family setting in Camrose and says "She (Leilani) complained of ill

*treatment by her mother and youngest brother, she says they both hit
her around. She is prevented from association with people, or leaving
the house ... She (Leilani) says she is sick and her parents refuse to let
her get the attention she needs." Mrs Clapson then indicates that "I
have had other occasions to deal with these people (the Scorahs) and
it appears to me that Mrs. Scorah attempts to destroy the confidence of
her children."*

*Undertaking #12: Respecting the drugs that were used on the Plaintiff,
while she was at the Provincial Training School: What was used, when
was it used, why was it used, and what were the results?*

Answers

*a) Drug - Stelazine (Trifluoperazine) Dose - 2 mg bid Dates -
October, 1958 to March, 1959*

*Reasons - To improve her loud, imprudent, often quarrelsome, and very
hard to manage behavior.*

*b) Drug - Phenobarbitone (Phenobarbitol) Dose - 25 mg qid Dates -
December, 1960*

Reasons - Administered for 3 weeks. No reasons given.

*c) Drug - Haldol (Haloperidol) Dose - 25 mg qid Dates - January,
1961 to April, 1961*

*Reasons - Started the day the Phenobarb was discontinued. Reason:
she has shown improvement in behaviour, but still becomes insolent and
defiant if she cannot have her own way. She wets her bed occasionally.*

*d) Drug - Haldol (Haloperidol) Dose - 25 mg bid Dates - April, 1961
to October, 1963*

*Reasons - The dose was reduced to 25 mg bid in April of 1961,
and then continued uninterrupted, until October 1963, when it was
discontinued. No reasons, other than quoted herein, were even recorded.*

These statements show that I was not just imagining or making up stories about how I was mistreated at home and drugged at the PTS. People in charge of me knew about this too.

*Undertaking #20: Produce the names of the literature that Dr.
Lampard knows of respecting the likelihood of low I.Q. being passed on
to a child.*

Answer

*a) Thompson, J.S. and Thompson, M.W. Genetics in Medicine 4th ed.
W.B. Saunders 1986 pgs. 3-5, 210-222, 271-272.*

*That book was by the same Dr. Margaret Thompson who was an
important Crown witness at my trial. She was regarded as an expert on
the topic. She was the only expert Lampard cited.*

DAY 13 (JUNE 28) A MIXED BAG OF GOVERNMENT WITNESSES

Gordon Gene Smith was a chartered accountant with a B. Commerce degree from the University of Alberta. He testified as an expert on income calculations in personal injury cases and made statements about the impact of living in an institution for the retarded on later income.

Leslie Leedman Peace was a private consultant in Lethbridge, Alberta and owner of Questioned Documents Investigations Inc. He was an expert on handwriting analysis. He testified about the handwriting and typewriters used in the various documents in my files. He concluded that Harley Scorah's signature on my admission form was forged by my mother.

Dr. Glennis Liddell had a Ph.D. in educational psychology from the University of Alberta. She worked at the Glenrose Rehabilitation Hospital doing psychological assessments. She reviewed my IQ test reports and school report cards for the trial.

DAYS 14 & 15 (JUNE 29, 30) MARGARET THOMPSON SHOCKS THE COURT.

Dr. Margaret Wilson Thompson had a Ph.D. in human genetics from the Department of Zoology at the University of Toronto. She was director of the genetic counseling service at University Hospital Edmonton from 1956 to 1962 and Assistant Professor in the Department of Genetics and Pediatrics at the University of Alberta at that time. She served as a member of the Eugenics Board from 1960 to 1962. She was not on the Board when they made the order to sterilize me, and she never met me. She did know a lot about how the Board operated and the kind of thoughts they had about children in the PTS. Although she was a Crown witness, I feel that most of the things she said helped my case. I was shocked, the judge was shocked, and people who read the news reports about her testimony were shocked by some of the things she had to say in 1995.

ON GENETICS AND INTELLIGENCE

Ms. Neudorf (Crown lawyer) Q: *Doctor, at the time you were on the board how did you define intelligence?*

Thompson A: *Well, intelligence is, I think, most simply defined as the ability to learn and remember.*

Q: *And what role does genetics or heredity play in acquiring intelligence?*

A: *Well, it's the overwhelming factor. Everything goes back to DNA.*

(trial transcript p. 1694)

LOWERING THE STANDARD FOR GENETIC DEFECT

In many cases the Eugenics Board ordered sterilization if they believed there would be a *"danger of the transmission to the progeny of disability or deficiency."* (trial transcript p. 1938). Danger means risk. It does not mean it will happen, but it might happen. The Sexual Sterilization Act section 6(a) actually used the words *"would result in the transmission of any mental disability or deficiency to his progeny."* The Act clearly requires the Eugenics Board to be certain that a disability would indeed be passed on to the children. That is a much higher standard than what they actually used. So many people were ordered sterilized who did not meet the standard in the law.

Anderson Q: So you applied a standard that was less strict than the Act, is that not so? You just had to find the danger rather than --

Thomspon A: A risk, yes. I agree that the statute could have been more precisely worded in that respect. (trial transcript p. 1939)

So the Eugenics Board when Thompson was a member was never wrong. The Sexual Sterilization Act itself was wrong. The Board did what it pleased, without asking elected representatives to revise the Act. They took the law into their own hands.

RAISING THE STANDARD FOR NORMAL INTELLIGENCE

In the 1950s, a "moron" was said to be a person who scored below 70 on an IQ test. That is what happened to me. I had only one test while I was at the PTS, not long before they presented me to the Eugenics Board. They said I scored 64 and therefore was a moron. Later Dr. Calder discovered my score was actually 71 in 1957. Would that have saved me from the surgeon's knife? Probably not.

When Margaret Thompson was on the stand, Sandra Anderson brought to her attention patient file 37-31 that was presented to the Board in 1961(see chart at the start of Chapter 12). The person scored 76 on an IQ test in February, 1961, just two months before the Eugenics Board hearing on April 14, 1961. They ordered steriliza-tion anyway. She also pointed out several other files where the IQ was above 70 but sterilization was the decision.

It happened that case 37-31 had actually been given four IQ tests over several years. In October of 1957 the score was 43, in March of 1958 the score was 57, in June of 1959 the IQ reached 64, and then in 1961 it hit 76. (transcript p. 1884). But Thompson decided that going from 64 to 76 was "not improvement into the normal range, unfor-tunately." (transcript p. 1889) So the person's IQ went up a lot, but the standard for being judged normal went up too. And the Eugenics Board did not wait to see if case 37-31's IQ would continue to rise.

GENETICS WAS NO LONGER THE MAIN CONCERN OF THE EUGENICS BOARD IN THE 1950S AND 1960S

Ms. Neudorf Q: When you were on the board from 1960 to 1962, what were the objectives of the board at that point?

Thompson A: By that time the purposes had really changed enormously … it was known … that the people concerned were very unlikely to be able to cope with the demands of raising children. And for that reason it [sterilization] was seen as a very useful social policy. For the protection of the people concerned. (trial transcript p. 1693)

A: My understanding was that first we thought about the risk that -- the cause of the patient's defect of disability was a genetic cause that had a risk of appearing in the offspring of that person. And (b) that even if there was no such major risk, that the person's ability to function as a parent should be considered. (trial transcript p. 1810)

A: But we were also concerned about the risk to the children of such a person in terms of their nurturing…(trial transcript p. 1823)

Anderson Q: Now, turning to the second part of the reason for sterilization given in the last example we were discussing. That's file 3595.

A: Yes.

Q: Also incapably of intelligent parenthood.

A: Yes.

Q: That means not fit to be parents or a parent in your opinion.

A: In terms of nurturing the child.

Q: Now, that wasn't in the Sexual Sterilization Act either, was it?

A: It says involves the risk of mental injury, either to such person or his progeny.

(trial transcript p. 1941)

Dr. le Vann's presentation of my case to the Eugenics Board in 1957 stated:

"REASONS FOR STERILIZATION: Danger of the transmission to the progeny of Mental Deficiency or Disability, also incapable of Intelligent parenthood." (Eugenics Board case #3280 presented November 22, 1957)

The Eugenics Board acted outside the law. They had no evidence at all that I carried any genetic defect. They decided to play God and decide who would be a good parent. They gave me no test of parenting ability. If they had, I bet I would have done really well. I believe that if they had followed the things said in the Sexual Sterilization Act, I never would have been sterilized. While living in Victoria, I was considered qualified to look after other people's children, babysitting as many as five kids at one time in my home, but the Eugenics Board decided I could not look after a child of my own. I loved children, and I wanted a child of my own more than anything.

ILLEGAL APPENDECTOMIES

The order for my sterilization said simply "*Salpingectomy.*" (Eugenics Board order dated November 22, 1957). But the summary of the actual operation on January 19, 1959 stated that I had "*BILATERAL SALPINGECTOMY AND APPENDECTOMY*" and that le Vann himself assisted in the operating room. The form calls this a "*Routine appendectomy.*" But it was not authorized by the Sterilization Act or the Eugenics Board, and there was no consent from my parent or me. Margaret Thompson saw nothing wrong with this.

Anderson Q: An appendectomy is not an operation for sterilization. Would you agree?

Thomspon A: That's true. It's -- in the case of female patients it's an operation that can very easily be performed without additional incisions and can remove a possible danger -- possible medical danger for later life. ...

Q: You agree that the Eugenics Board did not authorize appendectomies.

A: I do agree, but I would point out that the decision to perform an appendectomy was a medical decision that was outside the competence of the Board.

Q: Now in the operative reports there are frequent references to appendectomies being performed in conjunction with salpingectomy. Were you aware of that?

A: Yes.

Q: Did you ever question this?

A: No. There was no reason to.

(trial transcript p. 1944)

DOWN SYNDROME BOYS

Boys with Down Syndrome are always sterile. Margaret Thompson's own book on medical genetics stated that fact. But the Eugenics Board authorized vasectomies and a procedure called "testicular biopsy" for several Down Syndrome boys at the PTS. A biopsy is a surgical operation to remove a small piece of tissue. A testicular biopsy means a piece of a testicle is removed. For Case 3582 that was heard on May 22, 1960, when Thompson was on the board, the Eugenics Board authorized that kind of operation.

Anderson Q: And that tissue sample is not required in order to effect sterilization.

Thompson A: No, it's not part of the sterilization.

Q: Did it have some other purpose?

A: It might have had, but I would have no idea what the other purpose might have been.

(transcript p. 1953)

A: I have no idea why these biopsies were performed.

(transcript p. 1963)

Then there was case 3582 heard by the Board on July 27, 1960, which authorized Dr. Parsons to conduct an unusual operation on a Down Syndrome boy.

Anderson Q: Now, what operation was that?

Thompson A: A left vasectomy and a right orchidectomy.

Q: And what is an orchidectomy, Dr. Thompson?

A: It is removal of a testis.

Q: That is more than doing a biopsy, is it not?

A: Yes, it is.

Q: Do you know why Dr. Parsons would be performing an orchidectomy?

A: No, I don't know at all.

(transcript pp. 1956-7)

Sandra Anderson then asked Thompson to read a letter, exhibit 6, document D0146, that was a letter from Thompson to Dr. le Vann dated November 1961.

A: *This letter states: "The enclosed schedule for preparation of chromosomes from human testis is taken from Darlington and La Cour's test, The Handling of Chromosomes, 1960 edition. If it seems cumbersome, perhaps you would find it convenient to send us the material fixed in acetic alcohol and let us try the technique here."* (transcript p. 1960)

She then asked Thompson to read from exhibit 6, document D0147, a letter from le Vann to her dated November 28, 1961, in reply to her earlier letter to him.

A: *He thanks me for my letter and offer -- and my offer to help, as well as the for the squash method for preparing human testis, which I had sent to him. "I would be very pleased to take advantage of your kind offer to send material to you of any type for any research program which you may have scheduled, as well as the material which is slowly accumulating for the work with Mongols we are trying to accomplish at the school."*

(transcript pp. 1964-5)

The work was described in le Vann's own list of publications (document D0295A) as "A study of spermatogenesis in Mongols." (transcript p. 1965)

A: *Yes, now, biopsies would be required for that.*

So le Vann was doing research on how the testis of Down Syndrome boys fails to make sperm, and the Eugenics Board helped him by ordering testicular biopsies or an orchidectomy. Thompson did not seem to find this wrong.

Thompson A: Well, I don't think that the Eugenics Board was unaware, certainly in my time on the Board, that the probability of reproduction by a male Mongoloid was very slight indeed.

Anderson Q: So that it would not be necessary to sterilize male Mongols, would it?

A: It would in all likelihood not be necessary. On the other hand, I think you would agree that nothing would be lost by sterilizing such an individual. To make assurance doubly sure, as it were. (transcript p. 1974)

Her attitude made me so very angry. She thought it was OK to use those boys in le Vann's research project, to make them have an operation that was of no benefit to them but helped le Vann.

Judge Veit was not very happy with what she heard from Dr. Thompson. In her judgment she said the following:

> *"[124] I do not accept Dr. Thompson's evidence concerning the discussions that she had with Dr. le Vann regarding the taking of testicular tissue from vasectomized or castrated trainees: Both she and Dr. le Vann were conducting studies of "male mongols," males with Down's Syndrome. She gave Dr. le Vann detailed instructions about how to take samples of the tissue that resulted from the sterilization. In all the circumstances, this constituted encouragement to Dr. le Vann to use the trainees as medical guinea pigs. This is all the more repugnant because, from the 1940s on, Dr. Thompson and the board knew, as did all those involved in genetics, that male "mongols" are infertile: their sterilization was unnecessary."* (Veit, Reasons for Judgment, p. 17)

DAYS 15 TO 20 (JUNE 30, SEPT. 8-14) MORE WITNESSES FOR
THE CROWN

None of those Crown witnesses ever met me, interviewed me, or
gave me any kind of test. They read the reports of people who did
interview or test me, and they commented on those reports. I found
their time on the stand so tedious. Nothing they said showed that I was
in fact a moron. They were not able to show that the results obtained
by George Kurbatoff and Dr. Calder were mistaken. They questioned
how far I might have gotten in life without being sent to the PTS. I
have often wondered about that myself. I guess we will never know
for sure.

Brenda Gowan-Smith worked for Human Resources Canada as an
administrator of the Canada Pension Plan. She testified about disability
benefits and payments because of mental and physical disability.

Dr. Donald Walter Hepburn had a Ph.D. degree in educational psychology and was a consultant on schooling for children with special
needs. He was a special education supervisor for Alberta Education. He
also taught special education at the University of Alberta.

Dr. Thomas John Paton had an M.D. degree from the University of
Alberta and trained as a specialist in obstetrics in England. He was a
developmental pediatrician.

Dr. John Francis Keegan was a clinical psychologist who did psy-
chometric testing, including IQ tests. He had a Ph.D. degree from
Wayne State University and was adjunct professor of psychiatry at the
University of Alberta. He was employed by the Workers' Compensation
Board in Alberta.

The trial was finally over. I went back to live in Victoria for a few
months. I was totally exhausted and very sick. I was pretty sure we were
going to win the case, especially after Margaret Thompson testified and

shocked almost everyone with her attitude towards children in the PTS. But waiting for the verdict was very difficult. I could not return to a normal life until there was a verdict. I did not realize how, after the verdict was announced, my life would never be the same.

Chapter 15: *Ripples Across the Pond*

Against all odds and after many years of hard work by my lawyers and determination on my part, I became the first sterilization victim to win a case against the Government of Alberta. Justice Veit took almost two months to consider all of the evidence and arguments by both sides, then reach her decision. On January 24, 1996, my lawyers were told we would hear the decision the next morning at 8:30 AM before it was announced to the media and public at 10:30 AM. Sandra and Jon arranged for me to be in their office when we got the news. Oh my gosh, we laughed and cried when we heard! I remember making the sign of the cross and I thought, *Jesus thank you, it's over.*

The judgment was released on January 25, and a press conference followed at 12:30 PM. In the News Release issued by Field & Field Perraton that day, Jon Faulds said: "We are very glad our client has been awarded this compensation for the pain and harm she has suffered ... Her courage and determination since she began those proceedings more than six years ago paves the way for other victims of this law to claim compensation for the wrongs done to them."

I told the world that day: "What they did was wrong. They were playing God with the lives of thousands of people. This decision should make it easier for others who were treated like I was to come forward now and begin their own healing. I hope my fight is over now, and I can get on with my life." During the press conference itself, Jon, Sandra and I answered many questions from the media. One of my statements there was included in a documentary by the National Film Board of Canada: "They called me a moron, so what does that make them?"

The judge's landmark decision made some very harsh criticisms of the government. It was clear from her comments that the judge was appalled by what had been done to me at the institution. I was stunned, excited, and relieved, and I felt that her words completely vindicated me. I never dreamt that, by standing up for myself, I would make history.

Justice Veit's full judgment is many pages long and is part of the public record. This is her summary:

Muir v. The Queen in right of Alberta

Dominion Law Reports (4th series) 695

Court File No. 8903 20759 Edmonton

Alberta Court of Queen's Bench; Veit J.

January 25, 1996

Action for damages in respect of wrongful sterilization and wrongful confinement.

P.J. Faulds and S.M. Anderson, for plaintiff.

D.H. Lewis, W.C. Olthuis, R.F. Taylor and L. Neudorf, for defendant.

Veit J.:

Summary

[1] In 1959, the province wrongfully surgically sterilized Ms Muir and now acknowledges its obligation to
pay damages to her. However, the province leaves to the
court the determination of how much the province should
pay. The sterilization was irreversible; the testimony of Ms
Muir is supported by independent evidence and establishes
that the physical and emotional damage inflicted by the
operation was catastrophic for Ms Muir. This injury has
haunted Ms Muir from the time she first learned what had
been done, through to the time when she fully realized
the implications of the surgery. Her suffering continues
even today and will continue far into the future. The court
orders the province to pay her the maximum amount of
damages for pain and suffering resulting from the sterilization allowed by the law: $250,280 as of September, 1995,
adjusted to the date of issue of these reasons.

[2] The damage inflicted by the sterilization was aggravated by the associated and wrongful stigmatization of
Ms Muir as a moron, a high-grade mental defective. This
stigma has humiliated Ms Muir every day of her life, in
her relations with her family and friends and with her
employers and has marked her since she was admitted to
the Provincial Training School for Mental Defectives on
July 12, 1955, at the age of 10. Because of this humiliating
categorization and treatment, the province will pay her an
additional $125,000 as aggravated damages.

[3] The circumstances of Ms Muir's sterilization were so high-handed and so contemptuous of the statutory authority to effect sterilization, and were undertaken in an atmosphere that so little respected Ms Muir's human dignity that the community's, and the court's sense of decency is offended. Were there no other relevant factors, the court would order the province to pay punitive damages to Ms Muir, not by way of compensation to her for the harm inflicted on her, but rather as punishment to the province, of an additional $250,000. However, in this case, there are two reasons why punitive damages are not imposed. First, a large award has been made for aggravated damages; by itself, this award will be costly to the defendant. Second, the province voluntarily gave up what would have been a complete defence to Ms Muir's action: Ms Muir did not start her action soon enough. Had the province used this defence -- called a limitations of action defence -- that would have put an end to Ms Muir's claim. The effect of choosing not to use this defence is more than equivalent to an apology -- it constitutes a real attempt to make things right. As a matter of policy, government apologies and initiatives of this sort to redress historical wrongs should be encouraged; punishing governments for their historical behaviour would have the opposite effect.

[4] Ms Muir was admitted to the defendant's Provincial Training School for Mental Defectives on July 12, 1955, at the age of 10. She left the school, without having been discharged, and against the advice of the school's

administration, when she was nearly 21 years old, in March, 1965. The court finds that Ms Muir was improperly detained during this decade. The particular type of confinement of which Ms Muir was a victim resulted in many travesties to her young person: loss of liberty, loss of reputation, humiliation and disgrace; pain and suffering, loss of enjoyment of life, loss of normal developmental experiences, loss of civil rights, loss of contact with family and friends, subjection to institutional discipline. The court awards her an additional $250,000 for the damages connected with the detention, plus prejudgment interest from 1965 to the issuance of these reasons.

[5] Ms Muir claims additional aggravated damages of $125,000 relating to the detention because of the failure of the government's agents to adhere to the statutory requirements concerning admission, the use of school trainees, including Ms Muir, as human guinea pigs for drug research, the connection between the sterilization and the detention, and other abuse conduct. These elements of aggravation have already been taken into account in awarding aggravated damages for the sterilization. No award is made for aggravated damages in relation to the confinement because this would be a duplication of the earlier award.

[6] Ms Muir also claims substantial damages because, during the time she was detained at the Provincial Training School, the government failed to provide her with the

education and training that she might otherwise have achieved. While Ms Muir did have the ability to reach more than a grade 5 education, she has failed to prove that she has been, and will be, in a worse employment position as a result of the intervention of the province than she would have been had she remained out of the institution. As such, no award is made under this heading.

GLOBAL HEADLINES

By standing up for myself, I had sent a ripple across the globe, but to me, it seemed like a tidal wave. It was *such* a time. There was so much hype and attention! Reporters phoned me or contacted my lawyers asking to interview me. I spoke with so many of them that I lost track, but I kept many newspaper clippings, videotapes, and cassette tapes that serve as a record of the media's coverage. People appeared out of the woodwork, saying they were relatives. At one point, someone even found my unlisted phone number and called me, claiming they were a distant Muir relative and asking for money.

On March 10, 1996, I was thrilled to attend the premier of the NFB documentary, *The Sterilization of Leilani Muir.* The film is 47 minutes long and tells a very stirring story of my case, through interviews of me and other former PTS trainees. They used no actors. The video was shown across Canada and beyond, and it is still used in schools and universities to teach students about eugenics. On October 15, 2011 during the Alberta Eugenics Awareness Week, there was another public showing of the film at the main branch of the Edmonton Public Library. Graydon McRea, the film's producer, and director Glynnis Whiting joined me on a panel to talk about the film after the showing.

Fifteen years later, it still makes people think and talk about what happened at the PTS.

Other major news organizations sent reporters to get the story after the trial. The British Broadcasting Corporation (BBC) flew a crew of four people from the UK to interview me and others connected with the case. In 2003 French film producer Bernard Favre traveled to Alberta to interview me in my kitchen, as part of a TV documentary on the history of eugenics across the world, *L'Eugénisme : Bien né, mal né, loi et destinées* (translation: Eugenics: Well Born, Badly Born, Law and Destinies). My words were translated into French and shown as subtitles.

FINALLY, THE APOLOGY I ALWAYS WANTED

"Leilani Muir has the money, but she's still waiting for an apology from the Alberta government. 'I still want an apology and I'm going to go after it.' Muir said Sunday after watching a National Film Board documentary on her sterilization under the province's infamous Sexual Sterilization Act."

(The Edmonton Journal, Monday, March 11, 1996)

From the beginning of the lawsuit, what I wanted more than anything was to hear a personal apology from the head of the government. When I won my case, the government said nothing at all. They just paid the money and kept quiet. Soon after the NFB documentary was shown in Edmonton and reported in the media in March, 1996, Justice Minister Brian Evans told the *Edmonton Journal* that there would be no apology.

Then on February 20, 1997, an opportunity arose during a provincial election. Premier Ralph Klein was running for re-election. The British Broadcasting Corporation sent a film crew to Alberta to cover the election. The BBC crew found out that Klein was giving a campaign appearance at Northgate Mall in Edmonton and suggested I accompany them to the mall. They filmed me walking up to the Premier. Seeing us approach, his security guards tried to push me aside, but I stepped in front of Premier Klein and boldly asked, "Why didn't you give a personal apology to the sterilization victims in Alberta?", and he replied "Who are you?" When I told Klein I was Leilani Muir, he turned as red as a beet. I could tell from the look on his face that he knew who I was, and that he felt very embarrassed. He took my hand, patted it in a condescending way and said, "Oh, I'm so sorry dear." *Of course,* he tried to cover his butt while out in public during an election. What else could he have done? To me, that was the best day possible. Klein later complained to the *Edmonton Sun* that we set him up. So we did, and I think we did a pretty good job of it.

Sterilization victim receives personal apology from Klein

EJ Feb 20/97 A4

His gov't had no part in 'abhorrent' practice he tells her

MIKE SADAVA
and TOM ARNOLD
Journal Staff Writers

Edmonton

Premier Ralph Klein gave a personal apology to sterilization victim Leilani Muir Wednesday after she confronted him in a shopping mall.

Muir, 52, made headlines last year when Court of Queen's Bench awarded her $750,000 for having been sterilized without her consent when she was a 14-year-old resident at the Provincial Training School for Mental Defectives in Red Deer.

The operations were carried out on more than 2,800 Albertans from

Mario Pietramala, The Journal

Premier Ralph Klein offers his personal apology to Leilani Muir after she and a BBC television crew stopped him in a mall; at age 14, Muir was sterilized without her consent at a provincial institution

OTHER VICTIMS SEEK JUSTICE

During the trial and especially after news of my legal victory spread, many victims from around the world wanted to tell their own stories about forced sterilization. While the trial was still in progress, Donna Whittaker and Ken Nelson told the Edmonton Journal that they also planned to sue the government. During the trial itself, only Judy Lytton, Kitty, and John showed up. One or two of the others came to the courthouse, but they didn't enter the courtroom.

After the trial, more people *finally* started coming forward with their own experiences. Some of them no longer felt ashamed to talk publicly about their pasts. I was *so* glad to be able to help these other sterilization victims to stand up for themselves. My victory led to a flood of lawsuits filed by people who'd been sterilized in Alberta. By March of 1998, almost 750 victims had started sterilization suits against the Alberta government. Together, their claims added up to $764 million, or 6% of the government's annual budget.

The government was alarmed at the potential cost and did something really dumb to try to hold back the flood. On March 10, 1998, the government tried to limit the rights of sterilization victims to sue for compensation. Ralph Klein didn't feel his government should have to pay for the mistakes of previous governments. They introduced Bill 26, the *Institutional Confinement and Sexual Sterilization Act* that said claimants would be limited to $150,000 each, much less than my award. Even worse, it tried to prevent any legal challenges to the Act by someone citing the equal rights clause of Canada's Charter of Rights and Freedoms. If Bill 26 had gone forward, anybody who suffered from wrongful treatment at the hands of government—sterilization victims, gays, etc.—would not have been able to challenge the government. Fortunately, the introduction of the new bill was followed by such a public outcry, a real uproar by opposition parties in the provincial parliament that the government backed down the very next day.

Alberta Hansard for Legislative Assembly of Alberta, March 16, 1998 1:30 p.m.:

"MR. MITCHELL: Mr. Speaker, last week this government succumbed to opposition and public pressure to withdraw the worst piece of legislation in 27 years of Conservative government in this province. Bill 26 was so disgraceful in fact that a hard copy of the bill was not even presented to the government caucus prior to its coming to the Legislative

Assembly. The Premier did not trust his own colleagues
on this one, and he accepted, defended, and then rejected
the advice of his Justice minister to take away the rights of
703 very vulnerable Albertans. To the Premier: how can the
Premier say that he did not understand the notwithstanding
clause when he and his now lame-duck Justice minister
purposely neglected to give their caucus members a hard
copy of Bill 26 when they discussed it with the caucus prior
to bringing it to the Legislative Assembly?

MR. KLEIN: Mr. Speaker, the bill is gone. It is gone. We
will not be proceeding with the bill. Why does he want to
discuss something that simply is not going to happen?

THE SPEAKER: ... The hon. Member for Edmonton-
Norwood.

MS. OLSEN: My second question is to the Premier as well.
Can you please explain why it has taken over two years
and why over $2 million has been paid to Macleod Dixon,
yet the government has just started talking about settle-
ments?

MR. KLEIN: Mr. Speaker, let's not talk about two years. Let's
talk about 70 years. This legislation was introduced in 1928
and of course repealed in 1972. A lot of this only came to
light through the dispensation of the Leilani Muir case, and
that case prompted a number of others to come forward
and seek settlement or to pursue options through the court.

That is one of the reasons it has taken so long, that we
really didn't have to deal with these cases nor was there
any indication that we would have to deal with these cases
until after the Leilani Muir case was heard."

The other sterilization lawsuits went forward, and the government's attempt to trample the civil rights of sterilization victims made the history books. All of those lawsuits were eventually settled out of court, although the terms of the settlement were never made public. First those represented by the Public Trustee of Alberta settled. After that, 230 other victims represented by 10 lawyers decided to proceed to trial. The lawyers selected 17 plaintiffs to be test cases whose awards would set standards for all the others. The trial was scheduled to begin on September 7, 1999, but a settlement was reached before then. Newspaper reports on November 2, 1999, said that 230 victims were to receive $325,000 each. The deal allowed them to get compensation but not reveal their identities. In return, they were not supposed to reveal details of their cases.

TARNISHED REPUTATIONS

While some people were helped because of my court case, others lost their shining reputations. Dr. John M. MacEachran, who passed away in 1971, belonged to this second group. He had been chairman of the Eugenics Board from 1929 to 1965, and he signed the order to sterilize me. He was also the founder of the Departments of Psychology and Philosophy at the University of Alberta and had been the chairman of Psychology for many years. Long after MacEachran was gone, each year the Department of Psychology invited a prominent psychologist to visit Alberta and give a public lecture, the MacEachran Lecture. The special meeting room in the Department where Ph.D. oral exams were given was called the MacEachran room and featured a large oil painting of the old man.

Until the trial in 1995, most professors in the Department of Psychology did not know about Alberta's history of sterilization or MacEachran's big role in it. On September 15, 1995, after the testimony of witnesses in my trial was finished, Doug Wahlsten, a scientist who specializes in genetics and behavior, gave a speech to his department criticizing a book called the *Bell Curve* that claimed genes determine intelligence. He invited me to attend his presentation, and at the end of his speech he introduced me and asked me to give a brief summary of my experience with eugenics.

Doug and many others in his department were upset that MacEachran was still portrayed years later as a man of honour. They campaigned to have their long-departed chair's name removed from the conference room and lecture series. A vote at a department meeting made this change official. Doug later published an article that explained the decision to change the names.

"After a thorough discussion of several aspects of the question of honours and naming, on September 3, 1997, my colleagues and I voted 24 in favour, with one abstention, to rename the conference room and unanimously to rename the lecture series (Agenda and minutes, 1997). ... For the first time since 1975 the distinguished lectures (this time delivered by Charles R. Gallistel) were not held under the name MacEachran. When my student Katherine Bishop

had her Ph.D. oral examination in the conference room
on September 5, 1997, we took down the old portrait (of
MacEachran)."

D. Wahlsten (1999) History of Psychology and Philosophy
Bulletin, 10:22-25.

MacEachran had also founded the Department of Philosophy at
the University of Alberta, and every year that department awarded
MacEachran medals to its best students. The Department set up a committee to consider the ethics of MacEachran's deeds. They decided to
remove his name from every kind of recognition.

"The Committee faced the task of sorting out complex
historical events, influences, and standards; it also came up
against difficult issues of our ability to judge figures of the
past by standards of the present. Upon consideration of the
facts, however, the Subcommittee saw clear evidence that
the Eugenics Board, headed by MacEachran, acted unethi-
cally and unprofessionally not only by the standards of the
present but by the standards of its own time."

MacEachran Subcommittee (Kahane, Sharp, Tweedale),
Report of the MacEachran Subcommittee, Department of
Philosophy, University of Alberta April 1998.

MARGARET THOMPSON AND THE ORDER OF CANADA

In Chapter 14, Days 14 and 15 of the trial, the testimony of Dr. Thompson was quoted. Her words were widely reported in the media at the time, and many people, including me, were appalled at her lack of compassion for people in the PTS, especially those Down Syndrome boys who were partly castrated as part of le Vann's experiments. Her deeds and words have not been forgotten. In 2010 they came up again.

In 1985 Dr. Thompson was awarded the Order of Canada, a recognition of "lifetime achievement" that has "enriched the lives of others" (http://www.gg.ca). She certainly did not enrich the lives of children in the PTS. She helped to take away from many children something that was very precious, something God had given them. She got the award long before my trial, and I believe the people who voted for her did not know in 1985 what she had done in the early 1960s behind closed doors in Alberta.

In 2010 Mr. Rob Wells of Edmonton wrote to the Governor General of Canada, Her Excellency, the Right Honourable Michaelle Jean, asking that Thompson's award be revoked. Mr. Wells alleged that Thompson was responsible for "sterilization, mutilation and castrations for experimentation; serious attacks on human dignity and grave humiliation and degradation of human beings." He pointed out that forced sterilizations were regarded as serious crimes in the Nuremburg "Doctors Trials" that resulted in the *Nuremburg Code* of ethical conduct in medical practice (August 19, 1947). That *Code* requires "informed consent" of any person for any surgical operation. I was never informed about what was going to happen, and I would never have given my consent. Mr. Wells also mentioned that the *Rome Statute* of the International Criminal Court in The Hague, Netherlands, calls forced sterilization a crime against humanity. Wells also submitted portions of Justice Veit's judgment as part of his petition.

15.5 Article 7 of the Rome Statute of the International Criminal Court:

"For the purpose of this Statute, 'crime against humanity' means any of the following acts when committed as a widespread or systematic attack directed against any civilian population ... g) Rape, sexual slavery, enforced prostitution, forced pregnancy, enforced sterilization ..."

The Advisory Council of the Order of Canada reviewed the petition at its meeting in November of 2010, and on January 19, 2011, Darcy A. DeMarsico, Assistant Director, wrote Wells: "Following this review, the Council has decided not to pursue revocation of Dr. Thompson's appointment." They gave no reasons for their decision.

PART FIVE

A NEW LIFE (1996 ONWARD)

One of the first things I did after the trial was to claim my identity. I never knew my real dad, not even his name, but I did know that I wasn't Tom or Marie, Trainee #1325, or Exhibit C093, and I wasn't a Draycott or Scorah. I wanted a name of my own. I sat down one day and wrote a list of possibilities. One of them was Fitzgerald, because I always liked the Kennedys. I also liked the name O'Malley. Every year at Christmas, I loved to watch *The Bells of St. Mary's*. In the movie, Bing Crosby's character, Father O'Malley, says "Dial O for O'Malley" to the nun when she's sent away to a sanitarium. So I asked Lenora Harlton, my Victoria lawyer, to help me change my legal name. This is how I came to be Leilani O'Malley.

I'd been working for five years at the café in the Hudson's Bay department store in downtown Victoria when I had to leave for the trial. After it ended, I returned to Victoria, packed up my home, and moved to Edmonton where I worked at a gas station for the next five years. Although my finances were now secure, I didn't stop working. I liked being around people.

With more money in the bank than I thought I'd ever have, I was finally able to follow some of my dreams. One of the first things I did when I got my settlement was to pay back everyone I owed money. And I bought myself some pretty things, including a beautiful solid cherry wood desk with brass fittings. It was the desk I sat at while writing this book. I didn't know how to type, though, and had to teach myself how to use a computer.

FAMILY

I moved back to Alberta because almost everyone in my family lived there. I wanted so much to be part of a family. Of course, I could not have my own children, but my brothers had wives and children. Once I had money, they welcomed me into their homes, something they had never done before. I became Aunt Leilani, and I loved those children so much. For a time, I was happy in this role.

Soon after the award was paid to me, when I still lived in Victoria, I flew some of my nieces and nephews out from Alberta so they could join me for Halloween. I even rented a limo to drive them around in! It was such a time for me, spoiling those children and treating them like little princes and princesses.

Having money meant I could also make dreams come true for the people I loved. One of those was my brother's wife's sister who suffered from cerebral palsy. Cindy was a real sweetheart. Everybody loved her. She never complained, despite her disability, and she always had a smile on her face. She called me "Buddy." For years Cindy dreamed of visiting Disneyland. I was finally able to take her there. We all felt like kids at Disneyland, and I loved it. In the many pictures we took there, everyone was always smiling. We went on the "It's a Small World" ride three times. Cindy died a few years later. She has no more pain and is in heaven now.

FRANCE

My life changed in so many ways as a result of the court case. I made some good friends and traveled to beautiful places I never imagined I'd see. I'd come a long way since that first visit to the mental health clinic in Victoria in 1988. From that day on, I was ready to tell my story to the world. In Edmonton, Doug Wahlsten introduced me to Wim Crusio, a prominent scientist and expert on genetics working in Paris. Wim attended the first day of my trial and later made another dream of mine come true by inviting me to France. A handsome and soft-spoken man, Wim was born in the Netherlands. He is now research director of a lab in Bordeaux, France. For many years he was editor of the scientific journal *Genes, Brain and Behavior.*

After the trial, Wim invited me to speak at a scientific conference held in Orléans, France. Doug led the way. When we arrived in Paris in September of 1997 on the way to the conference, I couldn't believe I was really there. We walked up some steps from the train station, and there in front of us was the Arc de Triumphe! I looked around and said to Doug, "You'd better pinch me because I don't think I'm here." Locked away for most of my childhood, I remember arriving in Edmonton and thinking "This is a *big* world." But in Paris, I thought "O my gosh, this is such a big, *beautiful* world!" I never, *ever* thought in my lifetime I'd get to go to Europe and see a country that everyone dreams about going to. It was hard to believe that a person like me, who had never had an education, could see Paris, France.

When I was a child at the PTS, there was a nurse who had been to Paris and didn't like it because it was dirty. But I didn't find it that way; I couldn't believe how clean the city was! They swept the streets every day. They allowed dogs in restaurants. Little things like that make me happy, not the big things, but the ones most people take for granted. The truth is, I *never* take anything for granted. I treasure life and still haven't lost the ability to be amazed or awed.

On a visit to Notre-Dame Cathedral, I came upon Joan of Arc's tomb. It made me stop in my tracks. I had read stories about her, but to see her name there in the Catholic Church with all the other saints made it so real to me. I thought she must have been an angel for trying to help people like she did.

From Paris we took the train to Orléans. I loved that city, too. It was magical, just magical. We visited the old castle of Chambord, where people like Napoleon had lived. It was a beautiful place to visit, and I couldn't take enough pictures.

On September 29, 1997, I gave my speech at the conference. It was titled "Wrongful sterilization: a case history." Sitting in the audience that day was Jonathan Beckwith, one of the scientists who made history in 1969 by isolating a gene from a living organism. Imagine my surprise when, years later he described my presentation in a book he published in 2002.

"This looks like any ordinary scientific session: a large lecture hall, several hundred scientists sitting with pens and notepads, the speakers on the stage waiting their turn. At the podium, Leilani Muir of Alberta, Canada, begins her presentation before the 1997 meeting of behavior genetics and neurobiology researchers in Orléans, France. Muir, however, is not a scientist about to report her recent results. Instead, she tells a more personal story, one that brings tears to many in the audience, even those familiar with the history of the eugenics movement. Leilani's experience lends a heart-rending reality to this shameful period in scientific history. Muir cannot bear children. She was not born infertile. She was sterilized in 1959, at the age of fourteen."

(Beckwith. Making Genes, Making Waves: A Social Activist in Science. Harvard University Press, 2002)

The conference opened up a whole new world for me. I met many people there, like Don and Jeanne Nash. From the start, that wonderful couple made me feel *so* good about myself. Don invited me to speak at Colorado State University in Fort Collins, where he taught behavioral genetics. I took him up on his offer and visited him and Jeanne later that year. A highlight of the trip was driving with Jeanne up to the mountains to see the fancy hotel where they filmed *The Shining*.

Other friends who came into my life at that time were Dick Foley and Dana Middleton, hosts of a local television talk show in Seattle, Washington called *Northwest Afternoon – NWA*. After I appeared on their show for my first live interview, we became good friends. I've since spent a few weekends with Dick and his wife Mary in their Seattle home.

It meant so much to me not to be alone any more. Gone were the days when I felt I had nothing to say around other people. My world had grown many times over since I stood up for myself and stopped being afraid to speak out. More than once I've thought to myself, if my family could only see me now.

SPEAKING OUT IN ALBERTA

In the year 2000, a friend approached me to run for election to the Alberta legislative assembly on behalf of the New Democratic Party (NDP), a party I voted for as far back as I can remember. At the time, I was very upset and angry about cuts the government wanted to make in health care. I decided to run for politics because I wanted to oppose those cuts and help bring honesty to the government. In fact, my campaign slogan was "Leilani O'Malley. Tough. Honest. Committed." It must have struck a chord with people because, after I spoke in public, they often came up to me and asked why I was so honest. I'd answer, "What do you want in politics, honesty or lies?"

"As your MLA, my priority will be to stand up for Alberta families and make government listen. I promise to make sure the government gets its priorities straight in health care, education and other important areas." Leilani O'Malley

[NDP promotional brochure from the election campaign]

It was a good experience. In the March 2001 election, I earned 957 votes for three weeks of campaigning. During the campaign I was lucky to get to know Pam Barrett, an NDP member of the legislature for many years. She was a true champion of social justice and an inspiration for me. I was very sad to hear she passed away from cancer in 2008. I met other wonderful people during the campaign, including NDP leader Raj Pannu.

MORE PUBLIC SPEAKING AND COMMUNITY INVOLVEMENT

I've given many public talks over the years, trying to make people more aware of issues like child abuse, living with disabilities, and forced sterilization. I've lost count of the number of times I've spoken at conferences and events, but I'll never forget the experiences that touched me the most.

In Alberta, I've given talks for the Gateway Association for Community Living and the Edmonton Learning Community (ELC), both community associations that support people with disabilities. Since 2008, I have been speaking to the staff at Transitions five or six times a year, sharing stories of my life in the institution and helping them prepare to work with people with disabilities. So some good has come from the years I spent at the Provincial Training School.

Another project is the *Living Archives on Eugenics in Western Canada,* a CURA (Community University Research Alliance) project at the University of Alberta. A group of 30 people under the leadership of Professor Rob Wilson, including academic scholars and sterilization survivors like me, is involved in this federally funded five-year research project. We work with communities to develop accessible resources to shed light on the history of eugenics in Canada. I've been on the *Living Archives* board for several years and attend their meetings and conferences. I especially enjoy working with the university students and seeing their enthusiasm for documenting our troubled past in order to help keep the memories alive. They tell me how shocked and sickened they were when they first heard of the province's sterilization program.

Everyone seems to have a hard time believing it happened in our own province right up until 1972.

THE VAGINA MONOLOGUES

One of the speaking engagements that meant the most to me took place in 2009. The request came through Nicola Fairbrother, a member of the CURA Board. She asked me one day if I'd like to be in *The Vagina Monologues.* "*What* did you say?" I asked her. (I never use words like that.) Nicola explained that it was a play that shares the stories of women's experiences, good and bad. It was being presented by Pets Productions, and the Gateway Association, with proceeds going to Gateway and a local sexual assault centre. I thought about it for a day or two, then said "Yes." The part they'd chosen for me to read was about mistreatment of people in Africa. The organizers gave me 103 words to read. I practiced reading those words over and over until I felt ready. It brought back memories of acting in *Little Orphan Annie* when it was put on for the parents of PTS trainees.

The Edmonton production of Eve Ensler's *Monologues* was held at the Jubilee Auditorium on February 28, 2009. This time, I was joined on stage by local television and radio hosts, a city councilor and other amazing performers. I was nervous before the performance, but once I walked onto that stage, I felt at home. People told me afterwards I could be an actress! Well, I've had to act all my life. When I was younger, I couldn't show my fear or my tears to my mother. At the institution, I hid the fact that I was being starved every time I visited home. And, as an adult, I couldn't tell people where I was raised. Acting in *The Vagina Monologues* came naturally. Here are the words I read that day:

"Look out your window

The dead live everywhere

Think of your luxuries as corpses

Count the bodies

30 hacked children for Jed's new play station

20 tortured women so you can SMS photos from the part

50 amputated men, waving their missing hands as your sweet Andrew

mindlessly bounces his rubber ball

I held an eight-year old girl in my lap

Who had been raped by so many men

She had an extra hole inside her

When she accidentally peed on me

I was baptized

It isn't over there

The Congo

It's inside everything you touch and do

Or do not do."

[Words by Eve Ensler, *The Vagina Monologues*]

Chapter 17: *Cutting the Ties*

The government tried to compensate for the harm done to me and the others, and I'm thankful for this, but they could never pay us for what we lost. The damage continues. After the second round of lawsuits was settled, I traveled around Alberta trying to convince others to put their settlement money in trust so that they would have money for the rest of their lives. I wanted so much to help them. I had a lot of money one day and none the next. I didn't want this to happen to others. But it did—a number of them lost their money like I did to greedy people. All I ever wanted was a loving family. I found out the hard way that money couldn't buy this.

My brothers have always been like strangers to me. Even after I got away from the institution, I only saw them every few years. They didn't bother to tell me they were getting married. When I won the settlement, this changed. Along with the fake relatives, my own family came out of the woodwork and suddenly showed interest in me, the sister they never wanted. Hearing the stories of my abuse, my nieces said they couldn't believe my mother had done those things to me. But my relatives didn't ask me about the Provincial Training School, about what happened when I was young, or about the lawsuit. My brothers acted like they were glad I came forward, but they still didn't want to admit they had a sister. No way. They never introduced me to anybody, and I was never invited to visit with their friends.

Some of my relatives thought I had sued my mother. I told them I didn't sue *her*, I sued the government. "Does it say anything in the newspapers about that? Did you pay attention? It's the government I went after, not her," I said. Then they told me about a letter. Before the trial, government lawyers had written to my mother, and she showed the letter to my brothers. The wording in their letter made it sound like I was suing her, not the government. My mother died not long after that. I told my relatives, "See how things are twisted. You believed her all that time."

CHRISTIAN

I had always wanted a family of my own, and when my brothers and their families started to act friendly to me, I was grateful. I still wanted to believe they could be the family I always wanted. This was wrong, I found out later, but I wanted a family so much that I was blinded to their treachery. I thought I could buy their love. For a time after the trial, I bought them many things—groceries and other items. I gave three of my brothers money and loaned them even more when they asked. They said they'd pay me back, but they never did. My brother Christian borrowed more than $20,000. He said they really needed a new garage, so I paid to have one built for them. Even after my brothers sold their houses, they never paid me back. What I didn't give them, they stole.

I invested what was left of the settlement at the Royal Bank branch in Langford, BC. At the time, I was still living in Victoria, and I knew the manager there. He'd done a lot to help me when I didn't have very much money. Back then the bank had given me a loan to buy a car.

They'd put their faith in me, so I paid off the car loan and invested what was left. I was happy with that bank, but Christian hounded me to go to the Royal Bank with him to transfer my money to another banking institution. He bullied me into it, making me feel like I didn't know what I was doing, that I was inadequate. So, one day, we made an appointment and went there together. At the bank, my brother kept making me feel really small. On his directions, I instructed the manager to take my money from the Royal Bank and deposit it into an account at the National Trust. It was transferred directly to the other bank; there was no money order or cheque drawn up. That was the last I saw of the money.

I slowly realized there was no money left in my bank account when I began receiving notices for unpaid bills. The bank manager told me afterward that I should have never allowed my brother to transfer the money. I did what my brother told me to do, even though I was so mad that he was pressuring me. I wish so much that I'd made him sign a note with a witness. I was devastated at the loss.

WAYNE

I've never been more let down by anyone than my brother Wayne. He lived in Vancouver while I was in Victoria. Later, like me, he moved to Alberta after the trial. I had supported him since 1992. I bought him clothes and groceries. I gave him money, lots of money. I bought his cigarettes, paid his phone, cable, hydro bills, and his prescriptions. I let him use me to no end. I didn't see it until he finally moved in with me. That's when I woke up to all the lies he told.

After the settlement, I bought him $3,000 worth of furniture, nothing but the best. When he left Vancouver for Alberta, he told me he'd put the furniture in storage. I found out it was another lie when

I talked to a woman who said he'd sold all the things I'd bought him. The same lady told me it took four days to clean the apartment after he moved out; the place was in such bad shape that they had to replace the fridge. When Wayne moved in with me, he caused a lot of damage to my home. There were cigarette burn holes everywhere, even though I told him not to smoke in the house. When I came home at night from work, I opened the door to my house but couldn't even go inside because the cigarette smoke was so bad. I had to stay outside to catch my breath and leave the door open to air out the house. Whenever I'd open the windows, Wayne went around and closed them, even if it was the middle of summer. It was too cold for the bird, he said. He was such a filthy person. Here he was, staying at my place and not paying one red cent. He complained about the food and never even washed dishes or did his own laundry. When I was away at work, Wayne snooped around and stole anything of mine he could.

Why did I let my brother take advantage of me like this? While he lived with me, Wayne once said that he was very sick with cancer. I don't know if this was true. I did take him to the hospital one time for day surgery. Whenever I asked to talk to his doctor, though, he made an excuse, so I never knew what was really wrong with him. I have a feeling that he put on this 'sick thing' just to make everyone feel sorry for him, to get attention, so that he wouldn't have to go out and work. I genuinely felt sorry for him, and I loved him because he was my brother, just like I loved my mother for so many years.

But the nightmare of living with Wayne finally came to an end one day when the police came to my workplace. They asked me to visit the station so they could question me about my brother. I was horrified to find out that he had been writing letters to young girls and boys and inviting them to my home when I wasn't there. I was so angry when I heard this that I finally asked him to leave. After that, I had to sell the house and move into a smaller place. I never wanted to see Wayne again.

It didn't end there. I had stashed the few savings I had left in a small safe in my house. One day, when I tried opening the combination lock, it didn't work. I could not get into that safe. So I phoned a locksmith and asked him to come over and look at it. Not being able to open it, he had to drill a hole in the top. When we looked inside, there was absolutely nothing left in that safe. Nothing. I broke down and cried. The man asked me if I wanted to keep the safe. "What good will it do me to keep a safe with a hole in the top?" I asked him. I knew right away that my brother had stolen everything in it while he was living in my house.

When Wayne lived with me, I felt like a prisoner in my own home. But I stopped being a victim when I stopped caring for him. Slowly but surely, this is happening with the rest of my family. It took many, many years of being hurt and rejected before I decided I didn't care anymore what happens to them. I was always there for them, but not one of them has been there for me. I learned that when you have money, everyone is there with their hands out. But when the money is all gone, you're nobody to them. My family was ashamed of me, who had done no wrong, but now I am ashamed of them. Some are even criminals. I would not want to be in their place when they are called to answer to God for their deeds on Earth. Their minds were poisoned by my mother, and by a past I don't even know.

FORGIVENESS

People ask me if I've forgiven my mother for the way she treated me. As of yet, I can't say I have. I'd like to believe that something traumatic made her the way she was. I do know that when she was six years old, her mother died and left her and her sister alone. Maybe that's why she turned out like she did. I guess back in her day you weren't supposed to talk about what happened to you as a child or about the bad things in your life. I don't think she ever had someone she could turn to and talk with, or who could help her deal with whatever happened to her. Only God really knows. She's answering to Him now for what she did to me. Because I don't know the truth about my mother, or who my real father was, I'll never have closure until I reach heaven. And I'll never know why she didn't want a girl. If I did, maybe it wouldn't hurt so badly, and maybe I could forgive her.

I also wonder what my life would have really been like today if I'd had the chance to get a good education and have a normal family life in a loving home. As a survivor of child abuse, I look back and remember not knowing if I would ever get out alive and escape my home life. With God's help I did survive, and I did make it on my own.

Some things still make me feel stupid. I always try to do everything right the first time around and I try to be the best person I can. I used to feel unworthy of being around educated people, but not so much anymore. When I'm at speaking engagements or conferences, I tell others when I don't know or understand something. I know they accept this, but I don't always feel good about it. Sometimes, when I'm in a group, either I stand back and pretend I'm paying attention, or I walk around and make small talk with everyone. This too makes me feel small.

For many years, I suffered from post-traumatic stress. Because of my upbringing and confinement as a child and young adult, I don't function as well as someone who's lived in the outside world all their life, or in a loving home with a family. Sometimes when I see a happy family, which I still want, I cry for the mother and father I never had and would give anything to have. I've had two failed marriages and can't get a job that pays well. Because I was hidden away for 21 years, I spend as much time as I can by myself, hiding from everyone. This way I feel safe, that no one can hurt me. Even when I was married, I still felt alone.

Since I started speaking out, I've become a stronger person. Now I'm not so easily taken in. I'm told I'm a courageous woman for coming out and telling my story, but if I'm so courageous, why did I let this happen to me for so long? With the help of a few friends and medical people, I've worked hard to put my life in order over the past 20 or so years. I'm generally very optimistic about the future. Today, I own my own house. I dream about traveling around the world and teaching children to stand up for themselves. I don't worry as much about being perfect because I now know that there isn't such a thing as a perfect person. Everyone has a past and everyone has issues they must deal with.

One thing for sure is that I *never* quit. When I start something, I don't give up until I get it right, no matter how long it takes. I learned to be like this as a child, because I thought that, if I did everything right the first time, my mother would stop hurting me. Even though it never worked out that way, I still hung on. If I'd given up when I was a child, I wouldn't be alive, I wouldn't have left my mother, I wouldn't have started or won my case against the government.

I'm relieved to say that today I'm no longer a victim. I lived through a difficult experience and learned some hard lessons. I'm finally standing up for myself, and I'm proud of it. My brother, Wayne is dead, my mother is dead. What goes around comes around, I said to myself when I was in the institution. How did I know that? It came from within—from my strong will and from my belief in God. I thank Him for warm sheets and water, for no more beatings and no more being pushed down, and, especially, for my friends. God put me on this earth and kept me alive for a reason. Thanks to Him, I'm still here today to tell my story.

LASTING CHANGE

When I first started to write this book before my trial in 1995, I wanted to make sure that people learn the full truth about Alberta's eugenics sterilization program and never forget it. If we do not do a good job of teaching the next generations, all this could happen again. Now I am optimistic about the future. People have listened, and there have been some changes that I think will make a big difference for many years to come.

We were all thrilled when on October 14, 2010 newly elected Mayor Stephen Mandel of the City of Edmonton designated October 23 as the official "Remembering the History of Eugenics in Alberta Day." It will be celebrated on that day every year far into the future. At the ceremony at City Hall in 2010, I had the great honour to read the proclamation in public for the first time. We in Alberta are very fortunate to have a wise leader like Stephen Mandel.

News of the proclamation and the ceremony spread in the community, and before long a group of young artists led by Kay Burns decided to make their own mark to keep the memory alive. They had a brass plaque made that says "The Leilani Muir Footbridge," and they attached it to a footbridge crossing the North Saskatchewan River to downtown Edmonton. Gradually, more and more people have come to know about this, and the name has stuck.

Then in 2011, on November 14, the Canadian Broadcasting Corporation radio show *The Currents*, hosted by Anna Maria Tremonti, featured me in its series on "Game Changers." Ms. Tremonti recognized several people who created "moments that changed ordinary lives in ways we could not anticipate." She interviewed me by a telephone link to the CBC studio in Edmonton after arrangements were made by Gillian Rutherford. Her program was broadcast across Canada.

In 2012 my story grabbed the attention of Edmonton playwright David Cherios who asked me for permission to write a play based on my story. He then wrote a wonderful play titled *Invisible Child: Leilani Muir and the Alberta Eugenics Board*. *Invisible Child* was going to be the title of my book, but it was changed when we discovered another book with that same title had already been published. David was assisted in this project by my friend Lou Morin. The play was directed by Vincent Fortier, and Jenny McKillop played me. Actors Linda Grass and Randy Brososky had important parts too. All of them did a fantastic job, and they consulted me about several things in the play before it was ready for the big debut at the Edmonton Fringe Festival on August 17. The audience loved the play, and I joined the cast for a bow on stage after the show. I was just flabbergasted at how well they all did.

I was not the only one thrilled and impressed by *Invisible Child*. In May of 2013 the play won the Gwen Pharis Ringwood Award for drama at the Alberta Literary Award banquet. I was there with the cast, and we all had a great celebration. The play helps so much to keep the history of eugenics in Alberta in the minds of people in Alberta and beyond.

I want to end this book with words addressed to the entire country on *The Currents* show in 2011: "When I was born, God made me a whole person. When they sterilized me, they made me half a person. You never get over that hurt. You shower every day and you've got that stupid scar, because of what they did when I was 14 years old. Nobody has the right to play God with children's lives. This is why I've written the book and this is why I speak out. I don't want this to ever happen again to other children. My philosophy is that history repeats, but as long as I keep talking about it, it will not happen again."

PROCLAMATION

WHEREAS, the Living Archives on Eugenics in Western Canada project works to create a living archive of eugenics especially eugenic sterilization and associated institutionalization in Alberta;

AND WHEREAS, this project aims to produce awareness and provoke discussions about eugenics, disabilities and new technologies;

AND WHEREAS, understanding that the lives of people who felt the direct effects of eugenic laws and social policy are a crucial resource for our living archives and have much to teach us;

AND WHEREAS, through the Community University Research Alliances (CURA) grant, the University of Alberta's Department of Philosophy will work to facilitate the exploration of a difficult aspect of Canadian history into the collected history of eugenics;

THEREFORE I, MAYOR STEPHEN MANDEL, DO HEREBY PROCLAIM OCTOBER 23, 2010 AS "REMEMBERING THE HISTORY OF EUGENICS IN ALBERTA DAY" IN EDMONTON, ALBERTA'S CAPITAL CITY.

Dated this 14th day of October, 2010

Mayor of the City of Edmonton

Acknowledgments

The following people believed in me and were behind me one hundred percent. They made me feel that life was worth living. With wonderful people like these as friends, a person can't go wrong. Before I met them, I found it hard to trust anyone.

Dr. Mike Kovacs and George Nicholas Kurbatoff of Victoria, BC. Dr. Kovacs was the first psychiatrist who listened to me. He and George Kurbatoff, a psychologist, let me tell them the story of my childhood.

Lenora Harlton of Victoria BC, was the first lawyer who helped get my case started. She did a lot of work for me; phone calls, writing, and answering letters, and didn't charge a dime. If it wasn't for her, my case might not have gone forward.

Field and Field Perraton, the Edmonton law firm, now known as Field Law. They took on and won my wrongful sterilization case against the Alberta Government.

Myra Bielby of Field and Field Perraton, Edmonton. Myra was the first lawyer to take on my case in Alberta. She had to stop representing me when she became a Judge before my trial began.

Sandra Anderson and Jon Faulds. Sandra took over as my lawyer when Myra Bielby became a judge. She worked such long hours on my case, sometimes until midnight or longer and on weekends. Jon came in just before the trial. I couldn't have had two better lawyers.

Doug Wahlsten. I met Doug just before my trial, and he's become a true and loyal friend.

Dick and Mary Foley and Dana Middelton. Dick and Dana conducted my first live interview for their talk show in Seattle, Washington called *Northwest Afternoon*, and have become good friends.

The Alberta Association for Community Living (AACL) is the only organization that helped me with my finances before I won my lawsuit. The AACL should be credited for a lot of things they do for disabled people. They've helped to close many bad institutions in Canada. People with the AACL I'd like to thank are: Craig Shuller, Paul Kole, and Bruce Uditsky.

Glynis Whiting and her husband Ken. Glynis directed the 1996 Canadian National Film Board documentary, *The Sterilization of Leilani Muir*. She did such a wonderful job on this film.

Wim Crusio invited me to attend an international conference in Orleans, France. Thank You Wim, for making a girl's dream come true.

Don and Jeanne Nash of Colorado. When I met them in Paris, Don invited me to speak at another conference in Colorado. When I was there, I stayed with Don and Jeanne.

I also want to thank my friends who were there when I didn't have anything, and who helped me out so many times:

Sharron and Scott Hewitt from Victoria BC. Sharron and Scott were always there if I needed someone to talk to and helped me out whenever I needed someone.

Raulph Powell from Victoria BC. Raulph was like the father I never had. I met him and his first wife before she died of cancer.

Bobbie Jean was my roommate at the PTS in the 1950s. We became friends right away back then, and we met again after my trial. She's seen me go through a lot of changes, and I've seen her go through a lot also. Believe it or not, we're still good friends today.

Belle Parker My good friend Belle is no longer with us. She was one of the first people I met when I moved to Victoria in April of 1971.

Judy Lytton. This girl and I knew each other from the 1950s and 1960s, and we met again in 1995. Judy has a heart of gold. She's a very special friend to me and I'm glad to call her my adopted sister.

Lou Morin. I first met Lou when she was the manager of NeWest Press in Edmonton. Now Lou and her son, Evin are my good friends. She helped a lot with the book and also put together my web site. Without Doug Wahlsten and Lou Morin, I would never have finished the book. I am thankful for the many things Lou has done for me.

Rob Wilson. Rob is a professor in the philosophy department at the University of Alberta. I met him a few years ago when he asked me to speak to his students in a class he was teaching. Since then, we have become friends. Rob is now the director of the Community University Research Alliance (CURA) project known as the Living Archives of Eugenics, and he arranged for me to be a member of the CURA board from the community. There are about 30 of us on the board. A very big THANK YOU to Rob.

Thank you Dr. Wentz for bringing USANA products to the world. I know its helping alot of children and a lot of adults. I know for myself it is really working.

In 2010 I was invited to a meeting by my friend Jian at the Jasmine Garden Restaurant in Devon. This is where I met Carla Wilchuck and this is the night I decided to try USANA Health Sciences' products for one month only. After a week and a half I decided to stay on the products as I could already notice a difference in the way I felt. I swear by this product that it works and believe me, I was the most skeptical person in the world. Not any more. I went to the USANA International Convention in Salt Lake City and it was the best week of my life (besides going to Paris, France). THere I was honoured to meet the founder of USANA, Dr. Myron Wentz, and his son Dave. I even met the original Fred Flintstone, Bud Barth and Chris Gardner, who's struggle and success is depicted in the movie, "The Pursuit of Happiness". I'm honoured to be part of the USANA family.

Editor's Afterword *by Doug Wahlsten*

At the University of Alberta in Edmonton I taught courses in the 1990s on genetics and behavior. Most of us working in that field of science knew about eugenics, a scheme that was supposed to increase the average intelligence of citizens of a country. It was invented in England by Francis Galton, a cousin of Charles Darwin, and the eugenics movement spread to the United States of America where it was passed into law in several states. I had written scholarly articles and chapters in academic books criticizing the theory that genes we inherit from our parents determine our intelligences, but I had no idea that Alberta once had its own eugenics program.

One day in January of 1995 when I had just finished a lecture on genetics and intelligence, a lecture that mentioned eugenics, a student named Colin approached me and said his girlfriend's mother was working on a legal case involving eugenics. He gave me the lawyer's name, and on January 20 I sent Sandra Anderson a note expressing interest in the case. We corresponded, and then on April 4, 1995, she addressed my behavior genetics class and told us the whole sordid tale about Alberta's experience with eugenics. She later introduced me to Leilani Muir and I had an opportunity to speak with her before the start of the trial. I then attended as several days of the trial.

It was immediately obvious that Leilani Muir was no moron. She was mentally sharp, and she was angry at what had been done to her. Although I did not realize it at the time, she had started writing her book before the trial commenced. Soon after testimony in the trial was finished, on September 15, 1995, I presented a speech to the students and faculty in my department criticizing the arguments in a book called *The Bell Curve* that tried to make a case that class structure in American society was a natural consequence of genetic differences between rich and poor, white and black. Knowing the topic was very relevant to the theory of eugenics, I invited Leilani to attend, and I asked her to say a few words to my colleagues at the end of my presentation. I suggested she speak for about five minutes and try to tell everyone her story. This she did. With no rehearsal at all, in almost exactly five minutes, she gave them a succinct summary of her experiences with eugenic sterilization. I was very impressed, and so were most of my colleagues!

I had some contact with her after the case was decided in her favour, but mainly she tried to get on with her life. She moved from Victoria to Alberta, and we met from time to time. Then on October 18, 1998, we met and inspected all the documents from the trial, including the official transcripts, and made an index of everything, including her Provincial Training School records and letters from lawyers dating from Victoria. I advised her on a method for finishing her memoirs. We met again in 1999 and made an index of all her writings. By then she had completed 57 handwritten pages, each numbered 1-57, and had typed some of the material into a computer. We discussed an outline for her book and made a plan for further work. On September 23, 2000 we spread all of the documents onto tables and began sorting everything into categories.

The next time we met, she had written more material but was having difficulty typing everything into the computer. It was our good fortune to have a wonderful neighbour, Darlene Bernyk, who was good at computer work and was very interested in Leilani's story. Bernyk typed all of the hand-written material into a word processor program. Edyta Eansor then put all of this material into chronological order and made a first pass through the draft to do a bit of copy editing. She made notes on passages where important information seemed to be missing.

In 2007, all the typed material was assembled into one document and sent to Leilani for her review. At this time, she was working full time and could not do much writing. Writing had always been difficult for her, given the kind of education she had received at the PTS. But she sure could talk, and that is how we filled in many of the gaps in the first draft of her book. I made detailed notes on where things were missing or where there were conflicts between what was said in different chapters, then prepared a list of questions. I used a tape recorder and interviewed her. She is very good at speaking in clear, complete sentences. I therefore was able to type a transcript that was faithful to her own words, then cut and pasted the new information into the manuscript. In 2008, a complete draft of the book was ready for submission to a publisher. On January 9, 2009 we sent a prospectus to several Canadian publishers. In September of that year Leilani signed a contract with one of them, but suddenly in November of 2010 the publisher cancelled the contract.

After the contract was cancelled, Leilani and I began working with Lou Morin. Lou used the interview method very effectively and added more material to the book. She did some further editing and gave the manuscript to me for the final edits. I then worked closely with Leilani to tie up loose ends and update the more recent material. As is evident in Chapter 18, things kept happening, things that were very relevant to her story.

While the book was getting ready for final publication this year, it benefitted from a read and editing by Roger Brunt of Salt Spring Island, BC.

At the beginning of this endeavour, a crucial decision had to be made. Would this be a book about Leilani Muir or by her, a biography or an autobiography? There was never any doubt at all in her mind that this was to be her book, her story, her words. It was important that all editing of her words should leave the core of her writings and spoken words intact. The unique feature of this book is its first person account of the real impact on the life of a victim of eugenic ideology.

Much has been written about the thinking of those who founded the eugenics movement, got the laws passed, and set up institutions to carry out the orders from above. This is the story of a victim, an insider, a direct witness to abuse and injustice inflicted on her and many of the children she knew, someone who felt the sting of being labeled mentally inferior day after day for many years. Yes, there is a theory of eugenics, but her story tells how eugenics worked in practice, when all the noble words about science and progress are stripped away, leaving its core of cruelty and inhumanity plain for all to see.

Bibliography

PUBLICATIONS ABOUT EUGENICS IN ALBERTA

Baragar, C. A., et al. (1935) Sexual sterilization: four years experience in Alberta. *American Journal of Psychiatry*, 91: 897–923,

Caulfield, T., and Robertson, G. (1996) Eugenic policies in Alberta: from the systematic to the systemic. *Alberta Law Review*, 35: 59–79.

Chapman, T. L. (1977) Early eugenics movement in Western Canada. *Alberta History*, 25: 9–17.

Christian, T. (1973) *The Mentally Ill and Human Rights in Alberta: a Study of the Alberta Sexual Sterilization Act*. The Faculty of Law, University of Alberta, Edmonton.

Dickens, B. M. (1975) Eugenic recognition in Canadian law. *Osgoode Hall Law Journal*, 13: 547–577.

Finkel, A. (1989) *The Social Credit Phenomenon in Alberta*. University of Toronto Press, Toronto.

Grekul, J., Krahn, H., and Odynak, D. (2004) Sterilizing the "feeble-minded": Eugenics in Alberta, Canada, 1929–1972. *Journal of Historical Sociology*, 17: 358–384.

Henson, T. M. (1977) Ku Klux Klan in Western Canada. *Alberta History*, 25: 1–8.

le Vann, L. J. (1959) Trifluoperazine dihydrochloride: an effective tranquilizing agent for behavioural abnormalities in defective children. *Canadian Medical Association Journal,* 80: 123-124.

le Vann, L. J. (1961) Thioridazine (Mellaril), a psycho-sedative virtually free of side-effects. *Alberta Medical Bulletin,* 26: 144-147.

le Vann, L. J. (1968) A new butyrophenone: trifluperidol. A psychiatric evaluation in a pediatric setting. *Canadian Psychiatric Association Journal,* 13: 271-273.

le Vann, L. J. (1969) Haloperidol in the treatment of behavioral disorders in children and adolescents. *Canadian Psychiatric Association Journal,* 14: 217-220.

le Vann, L. J. (1971) Clinical comparison of haloperidol and chlorpromazine in mentally retarded children. *American Journal of Mental Deficiency,* 75: 719-723.

MacEachran, J. M. (1932) A philosopher looks at mental hygiene. *Mental Hygiene,* 16: 101-119.

MacLean, R. R., and Kibblewhite, E. J. (1937) Sexual sterilization in Alberta: eight years' experience, 1929 to May 31, 1937. *Canadian Public Health Journal,* 587-590.

McLaren, A. (1990) *Our Own Master Race: Eugenics in Canada 1885-1945.* McClelland and Stewart, Toronto.

McWhirter, K. G., and Weijer, J. (1969) The Alberta Sterilization Act: a genetic critique. *University of Toronto Law Journal,* 19: 424-431.

National Film Board of Canada, Montréal. (1996) *The Sterilization of Leilani Muir.* (public broadcast on "Witness," Canadian Broadcasting Corporation TV, March 12, 1996)

Park, D. C., and Radford, J. P. (1998) From the case files: reconstructing a history of involuntary sterilization. *Disability & Society,* 13: 317-342.

Pocock, H. F. (1932/33) Sterilization in the Empire. *Eugenics Review,* 24: 127-129.

Powers, D. (1979) Sterilization law 'reminiscent' of Nazi Germany. *Edmonton Journal*, Feb. 17, p. B2.

Pringle, H. (1997) Alberta barren. *Saturday Night*, 112 (5): 30-74.

Puplampu, K. P. (2008) Knowledge, power, and social policy: John M. MacEachran and Alberta's 1928 Sexual Sterilization Act. *Alberta Journal of Educational Research*, 54: 129-146.

Sexual Sterilization Act, 1928. Statutes of Alberta, Chapter 37.

Sexual Sterilization Act, 1942. Revised Statutes of Alberta, Chapter 194.

Wahlsten, D. (1979) A critique of the concepts of heritability and heredity in behavioral genetics. In J. R. Royce and L. Mos (Eds.), *Theoretical Advances in Behavioral Genetics*. Sijthoff and Noordhoff, Alphen aan den Rijn, The Netherlands, pp. 425-481.

Wahlsten, D. (1995) Increasing the raw intelligence of a nation is constrained by ignorance, not its citizen's genes. *Alberta Journal of Educational Research*, 41: 257-264.

Wahlsten, D. (1997) Leilani Muir versus the Philosopher King: eugenics on trial in Alberta. *Genetica*, 99: 185-198.

Wahlsten, D. (1999) The eugenics of John. M. MacEachran warrant revocation of honours. *History of Psychology and Philosophy Bulletin*, 10: 22-25.

Wahlsten, D. (2002). The theory of biological intelligence: history and a critical appraisal. In R. Sternberg and E. Gigorenko (eds.), *The General Factor of Intelligence: How General Is It?* Mahwah, NJ: Erlbaum, pp. 245-277.

Wallace, R. C. (1934) The quality of the human stock. *Canadian Medical Association Journal*, 31: 427-430.

HISTORICAL STUDIES OF EUGENICS ELSEWHERE

Allen, G. E. (1995) Eugenics comes to America. In *The Bell Curve Debate. History, Documents, Opinions*, edited by R. Jacoby and N. Glauberman, Times Books, New York .

Chase, A. (1977) *The Legacy of Malthus. The Social Costs of the New Scientific Racism*. Knopf, New York.

Chorover, S. L. (1979) *From Genesis to Genocide*. MIT Press, Cambridge, Massachusetts.

Devlin, B., Fienberg, S. E., Resnick,D. P., and Roeder, K.. (1995) Galton redux: eugenics, intelligence, race, and society: a review of *The Bell Curve: Intelligence and Class Structure in American Life*. *Journal of the American Statistical Association*, December, 1483-1488.

Ferster, E. Z. (1966) Eliminating the unfit - Is sterilization the answer? *Ohio State Law Journal*, 27: 591-633.

Gould, S. J. (1996) *The Mismeasure of Man*. Norton, New York.

Kevles, D. J. (1985) *In the Name of Eugenics: Genetics and the Uses of Human Heredity*. Knopf, New York.

Langdon-Down, R. (1926/27) Sterilization as a practical policy. *Eugenics Review*, 18: 205-210.

Lerner, R. M. (1992) *Final Solutions. Biology, Prejudice, and Genocide*. Pennsylvania State University Press, University Park.

Lombardo, P. A. (2008) *Three Generations. No Imbeciles. Eugenics, the Supreme Court, and Buck v. Bell*. Johns Hopkins University Press, Baltimore.

Meyer, J.-E. (1988) The fate of the mentally ill in Germany during the Third Reich. *Psychological Medicine*, 18: 575-581.

Myerson, A., Ayer, J. B., Putnam, T. J., Keeler, C. E., and Alexander, L. (1936) *Eugenical Sterilization. A Reorientation of the Problem*. Macmillan, New York.

Thom, D., and Jennings, M. (1996) Human pedigrees and the 'best stock': from eugenics to genetics? In *The Troubled Helix: Social and Psychological Implications of the New Human Genetics*, edited by T. Marteau and M. Richards, Cambridge University Press, Cambridge.

MAJOR EVENTS BY YEAR AND DAY [CODE IN BRACKETS IS
EXHIBIT NUMBER AT THE TRIAL]

1941	Amy Novakowski and Mr. Draycott are married
1942	Draycott joins Canadian Armed Forces and goes overseas
1943	Amy and Harley begin living together. She uses his name.
1944, July 15	Leilani Marietta Draycott is born in Calgary, Alberta [A001]
1950, April	Dr. le Vann publishes article in *Amer. J. Mental Deficiency* that says mentally deficient children are like another species, not fully human
1951, Sept.	LM starts grade 1 in Niobe, AB, at age 7 years
1951, Oct.	Calgary Guidance Clinic diagnostic summary of LM [A003a]
1951, Oct.	Letter from Le Vann to Dr. Galloway about LM [A003b]
1952, Nov. 16	LM put into Lacombe Home and convent for over one month
1953, Feb. 14	Municipality of Black Diamond approves admission of LM to PTS [A010]
1953, Feb. 18	Application for PTS admission of LM signed by "H. G. Scorah" [A039]

1953	LM admitted to Holy Cross Hospital with ulcers on arm
1954	LM starts grade 1 in Priddis, AB (3 years after Niobe)
1955, May 9	LM put into the Lacombe Home for two months
1955, June 16	Municipality of Foothills approves admission of LM to PTS [A023]
1955, June 28	Le Vann writes Mrs. Scorah about LM [A025]
1955, July 12	Admission of LM to PTS [A027-29]
1955, July 12	Consent for sterilization of LM signed (forged) by Amy "Scorah" [A031]
1955, July 16	Le Vann himself signs physician's certificate required for admission
1955, Dec. 15	Le Vann writes Provincial Guidance clinic about IQ test of LM [A056]
1955, Dec. 20	Provincial Guidance clinic replies that no IQ test was given [A057]
1957, Feb. 20	Margaret Thompson writes to Le Vann [D0104]
1957, Nov. 22	Presentation of LM to Eugenics Board; sterilization ordered [A105-108]
1959, Jan. 19	Operation (salpingectomy and appendectomy) done on LM [A128-132]
1960	Mr. Draycott killed in auto accident; LM not told of it
1960, July 26	PTS asks Scorahs if they have abandoned LM [A163-166]

1961, Aug. 27	Mrs. McWilliams writes to PTS; wants to adopt LM [A167]
1961	Letters between Thompson and Le Vann re Down Syndrome [D0146-148]
1962, Nov. 21	Mrs. Hepner writes to Le Vann about abuse of LM at home [A244]
1962, Dec. 7	Mrs. Alford memo to Le Vann about mistreatment of LM at home [A250]
1963, Oct. 2	Le Vann writes memo proposing to discharge LM [A273]
1963, Oct. 3	Discharge is cancelled [A274]
1963, Oct. 4	Clapson, welfare officer of Camrose, writes Le Vann about abuse of LM
1964, July 31	Mrs. Alford, social worker, writes Le Vann re visit to Scorah home [A318]
1964, Nov. 30	Marriage of Harland Scorah and Amy [A322b]
1965	John MacEachran retires from Eugenics Board; served since 1929 [X12]
1965, Mar. 9	LM is taken from the PTS by her mother; not a discharge
1965, Mar. 10	Le Vann memo calls this a discharge [A338]
1965, Mar. 12-25	Letters by Amy, LM, Le Vann re discharge [A339-343]
1965, June 8	Final letter from Le Vann to LM [A348]
1965	Harley and Amy separate
1965	LM leaves mother's apartment in Edmonton, lives on her own; takes photos at bus station

1966	LM works 6 months as ward aid at Edm. General Hospital
1966, April	LM sees Dr. Hulley at U of Alberta hospital about her surgery at PTS
1966, April 29	Hulley writes Le Vann to get details of the surgery [C001]
1966, May	Letters to and from Le Vann and U of A hospital [C003-7]
1966, June 29	Le Vann writes to Dr. Parsons at U of A hospital about operation [C008]
1966, Aug. 12	U of Alberta hospital prepares summary of LM case [C009]
1966-68	LM works as waitress at Smitty's for two years
1968, Nov.	LM marries Bill Yuckshyn; discovers Draycott, not Scorah, was father
1969, April	Blair Report on mental health in Alberta; questions eugenics [D0014]
1969, Summer	LM moves to Yellowknife to take waitress job; stays 3 months
1969	Moves back to Calgary; baby sitting job and harassment
1969, Nov.	LM divorces Bill Yuckshyn
1970	LM moves to Vancouver, BC, works at the Purple Steer
1970	LM moves to Quesnel, BC
1971, April	LM moves to Victoria, BC
1971, October	LM sees Dr. Dickson, who confirms she had laparotomy and tubal sugery

1971, Oct.4,12	Dickson writes Le Vann about surgery [C011–013]
1972, June 2	Sexual Sterilization Act repealed [D0289]
1974, June 5	Dr. Graham-Marr tries to rejoin LM's fallopian tubes [C014]
1975, Sept. 8	Psychiatrist Dr. McTavish interviews LM [C015]
1976, Dec. 8	Dept. of Veterans Affairs writes LM re Draycott [C016]
1978	LM meets Darren Muir in Victoria
1979, Feb.–Mar.	Drs. Weir, Rippington write to Dr. Zedel re LM's tubes [C020–022]
1979, Feb. 17	Edmonton Journal article by Dan Powers on Eugenics Board
1980, March	Last exploratory surgery to examine LM's fallopian tubes
1980, May 2	LM marries Darren Muir in Victoria
1980, May–Dec.	Letters from Drs. Rippington, Gomel to Drs. Zedel and Prevost [C024–27]
1981, Jan. 16	Dr. Zedel's history of LM case; sterilization cannot be reversed [C028]
1981	LM has hysterectomy [C030]
1982	Muirs apply to adopt a child
1984	Adoption is rejected because LM was resident of the PTS
1984, April 4	Lawyer Hunter writes to Alberta Social Services, and Alberta Ombudsman re LM; tries to get PTS files [C031–033]

1984, Apr.-Aug.	Letters back and forth among Hunter, McCormick, LM [C034-043]
1984, Aug. 24	LM's brother kills three people in Delta, BC
1984, Dec. 11	AB, BC Ombudsmen write to LM, not lawyer [C044-5]
1985, Feb.-Apr.	More letters from AB Ombudsman to LM, who is trying to get her PTS files [C046-049]
1986, August	Leilani and Darren Muir separate
1988, Feb. 5	Alberta Ombudsman writes to LM [C053-054]
1988, May	Divorce from Darren Muir
1988, Aug. 11	Alberta Attorney General Zinger writes LM about PTS files [C056]
1988, Oct. 24	Lawyer Lenora Harlton, representing LM, writes McCormick and Zinger [C059-061]
1988, Nov. 4, 9	McCormick and Zinger write to Harlton [C063, 065]
1988, Dec.	Poem "Who is My Friend" written in Victoria
1988, Dec.	West Communities Mental Health does assessment of LM [C068-070]
1988, Dec.	Interview with Dr. Kovacs in Victoria
1989, Jan. 27	Harlton writes Alberta Ombudsman [C073]
1989, Feb. 24	Kurbatoff gives LM a WAIS IQ test; score is 87 [C072]
1989, June 22	Myra Bielby in Edmonton becomes LM's lawyer
1989, June 29	Field & Field law firm in Edmonton writes to AB attorney general [C073]

1989, Jun.–Nov.	Letters between Bielby of Field & Field and McCormick [C074–082]
1989, Nov. 6	Bielby files Statement of Claim
1989, Nov. 8	LM gets WAIS IQ test, WRAT test by Lyons; talks with Calder [C083-4]
1989, Nov.– Dec.	McCormick, Calgary General Hospital, writes to Bielby [C085, 088]
1990, Sept.18,19	Examination for Discovery of LM and Lampard by Bielby
1991, April	Bodner becomes LM's lawyer after Bielby becomes a judge
1991, June 5	Continuation of Examination for Discovery of Lampard
1992, Jan. 10	Continuation of Exam. for Discovery of Lampard, LM
1992, June 15	Continuation of Exam. for Discovery of Lampard
1993, January	Vocational testing of LM in Edmonton by Dr. Roy Brown
1993, June 8	First news articles about LM lawsuit; Victoria Times–Colonist and Edmonton Journal (article by Deborah Pearce); LM has started book
1993, Sept. 3	Continuation of Examination for Discovery of Muir
1995, Feb. 9	LM given WRAT test by Conway [C094]
1995, Feb. 23	Cara Brown gives expert opinion about LM earnings [X43]

1995, Feb. 23	Dr. Robertson expert report on Alberta Eugenics Board [X75]
1995, Feb. 25	Leslie Peace expert report on hand writing of Scorahs [X95]
1995, May 8	Dr. Copus submits report based on interview of LM [X41]
1995, May 26	Lyons IQ test of LM is rescored by Calder [X32]
1995, May 29	Trial scheduled to begin; postponed after ski accident of Crown lawyer
1995, June 7	Report by Liddell, critique of LM tests [X94]
1995, June 12	Trial begins; Alberta government admits liability for sterilization
1995, Jun.13–30	Many witnesses testify
1995, June 16	Edmonton Journal reports Whittaker and Nelson lawsuits
1995, July 1	LM returns to Victoria during trial recess
1995, Sept. 8–14	More witnesses; Keegan
1995, Sept. 15	LM speaks at U of Alberta psychology colloquium; her first public speech
1995, Nov.	Written arguments by Plaintiff, Defendant submitted
1995, Dec.	Lengthy reply by Defendant to argument of Plaintiff; government proposes to pay LM a settlement of $60,000 for sterilization
1996, Jan. 7	AB Association for Community Living calls for compensation for other sterilization victims

1996, Jan. 25	Madame Justice Veit announces her decision and reasons
1996, Jan. 26	John Tomyn will sue for damages; Allan Garber is lawyer
1996, Jan. 27	Madeleine Shipitski says she will also sue
1996, Feb. 14	Justice Veit orders govt .to pay LM $230,000 legal costs
1996, Feb. 28	Alberta government pays LM $973,000
1996, Mar. 1	More than 30 victims are represented by Field & Field Perraton
1996, Mar. 4	Edmonton Journal announces LM "still wants gov't apology"
1996, Mar. 12	National Film Board documentary on LM case on CBC-TV
1996, Mar. 13	Justice Minister Brian Evans says there will be no apology
1996, Dec. 3	Nearly 700 former inmates of PTS are suing the government
1997, Feb. 20	Premier Ralph Klein gives LM a personal apology
1997, Mar. 23	Article in *Guardian Weekly* about LM
1997, June	Article "Alberta Barren" by Heather Pringle in *Saturday Night*
1997, Sept. 3	U of Alberta psychology department votes to remove MacEachran's name from invited lecture series and award
1997, Sept.	LM addresses French–American Summer School in France

1997, Oct. 1	*La Republique du Centre* article: "Une Canadiene steriliseé de force à 14 ans"
1997, Oct. 20	Filming of "Heart of the Sun" in Edmonton; based on Betty Lambert play about woman sterilized in Alberta in the 1930s
1998, Mar. 10	Bill 26 seeks to limit compensation and right to sue for sterilization victims; withdrawn the next day
1999, Mar. 16	Lawyers representing 17 test claimants are ready to go to trial on September 7, 1999; government is raising limitation as defence
1999, Apr. 25	"Heart of the Sun" wins award at Alberta Film and TV Awards ceremony
1999, Nov. 2	Out of court settlement; government will pay 230 victims $325,000 each
2001, Feb. 18	LM to run as New Democrat candidate in Leduc riding
2003, June 19	Old PTS administration building struck by lightning; destroyed
2009	Researchers in Western Canada and former victims of sterilization are awarded SSHRCC grant for Community-University Research Alliance project on "Living Archives of Eugenics"
2010, Oct. 23	Mayor Stephen Mandel proclaims this as "Remembering Eugenics in Alberta Day"

2011, Nov. 14	LM is interviewed by Anna Maria Tremonti on CBC Radio show "The Currents" and designated a "Game Changer"
2012, May	Muir's website leilanimuir.ca with a blog is up and running.
2012, Aug. 17	The play *Invisible Child* based on Muir's story is performed at the Edmonton Fringe Festival.
2013, May	The play *Invisible Child* wins the Gwen Pharis Ringwood Award for drama at the Alberta Literary Award banquet.